W9-DEW-463

Praise for

The Retirement Catch-Up Guide

"This book offers great advice for baby boomers and anyone else concerned with retirement planning."
—Senator Chuck Grassley
Former Chairman, Senate Special Committee on Aging

"One of the most realistic finance writers around...If you live outside the cookie cutter of American financial life, don't despair: there are lots of nontraditional suggestions here."
—*The Dallas Morning News*

"A jam-packed guide filled with commonsense advice, countless resources, and personal anecdotes that make the task of planning for retirement much less daunting. Ellen Hoffman understands the complexities of retirement planning, and her gift is the ability to convey the information in the most basic and compelling manner."
—Don Blandin
President, American Savings Education Council

"Easy reading...Most of the advice is top-rate, solid, and original...There's an excellent list of resources that anyone, no matter what age, will find helpful."
—*USA Today*

"If you haven't started saving yet for retirement, this book will help you find the incentive to do so."
—Ric Edelman
Edelman Financial Center

ABOUT THE AUTHOR

Ellen Hoffman is the retirement columnist for Business Week Online and was the Washington columnist for *Money Magazine*'s former newsletter, *Retire With Money*. Her articles on retirement and personal finance have appeared in *Business Week*, *Reader's Digest, Money Magazine, Modern Maturity*, and many other publications. She has appeared on NBC's "Today Show," CNBC, and Fox News, as well as many other TV and radio shows to talk about retirement issues, and is a popular speaker and workshop presenter. Hoffman has served on the staff of the U.S. Senate, where one of her specialties was issues affecting the elderly. Ms. Hoffman helped found the Professional Business Women's Association in the area where she lives. She has also served on a Presidential advisory committee on women's education and a committee that advised the Secretary of Health, Education and Welfare on a broad range of issues affecting women.

She is the author of *Bankroll Your Future: How to Get the Most from the Government for Your Retirement Years* and *The Retirement Catch-Up Guide: 54 Real-Life Lessons to Boost Your Future Resources Now!*, both from Newmarket Press. For more information on retirement planning, see the author's website at www.retirementcatchup.com. Ms. Hoffman lives near Washington, D. C.

The
RETIREMENT
Catch-Up Guide

54 *Real-Life Lessons to Boost Your Retirement Resources Now!*

Ellen Hoffman

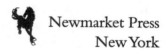
Newmarket Press
New York

This book is dedicated to the scores of people—friends, business colleagues, friends of friends, and total strangers—who graciously shared their highly personal stories and even financial information with me. I hope they find that this book is not only *about* them but also *for* them.

Copyright © 2002, 2000 by Ellen Hoffman
All rights reserved. This book may not be reproduced, in whole or in part, in any form, without written permission. Inquiries should be addressed to Permissions Department, Newmarket Press, 18 East 48th Street, New York, NY 10017.
This book is published in the United States of America and Canada.

10 9 8 7 6 5 4 3 2

Library of Congress Cataloging-in-Publication Data
Hoffman, Ellen, 1943–
    The retirement catch-up guide : 54 real-life lessons to boost your retirement resources now / Ellen Hoffman.
        p. cm.
    Includes index.
    ISBN 1-55704-518-6
    1. Retirement income—United States—Planning—Handbooks, manuals, etc. 2. Retirement—United States—Planning—Handbooks, manuals, etc. 3. Retirees—United States—Finance, Personal—Handbooks, manuals, etc. I. Title.
    HG179 .H5925 2000
    332.024'01dc21   00-036147

Quantity Purchases: Companies, professional groups, clubs, and other organizations may qualify for special terms when ordering quantities of this title. For information, write Special Sales Department, Newmarket Press, 18 East 48th Street, New York, NY 10017; call (212) 832-3575 or (800) 669-3903; fax (212) 832-3629; or e-mail sales@newmarketpress.com.
www.newmarketpress.com

Designed by Mercedes Everett
Manufactured in the United States of America

NOTE TO THE READER

This publication is designed to provide accurate and authoritative information in regard to the subject matter covered. It is published with the understanding that the publisher and author are not engaged in rendering legal, accounting, or other professional services. If legal advice or other professional advice, including financial, is required, the services of a competent professional person should be sought.

CONTENTS

INTRODUCTION

If it was ever time for Americans to catch up on saving for retirement, that time was in the dawning months of 2002.

The collapse of the tech stock boom a couple of years earlier had dealt a body blow to thousands, if not millions, of retirement accounts. The slowing economy, wounded further by the terrorist attacks of September 11, 2001, became even more lethargic. Hundreds of thousands of workers lost their jobs, and along with their employment, they lost matching contributions to their 401(k)s. For the jobless, paying the rent, food, and utility bills had to take priority over saving for retirement. Enron employees who had invested large portions of their 401(k) in company stock watched helplessly as the stock value tumbled from over $84 per share early in 2001 to as low as 25 cents as the year ended.

Fortunately, as 2002 dawned, something happened that offered pre-retirees at least the hope of benefiting from their mistakes and recuperating from setbacks to their retirement savings: **Uncle Sam made catching up on your retirement savings a national goal.** On January 1, 2002, new federal tax changes offering financial incentives to save more for retirement over the next several years began to take effect. The changes came in what the financial world now calls "EGTRRA," the "Economic Growth and Tax Relief Reconciliation Act of 2001." The new law provides several important incentives that make it possible for almost everyone to step up their retirement savings:

- Higher limits on tax-deferred contributions to your 401(k) or other retirement accounts at work
- Higher limits on contributions to both traditional, tax-deferred IRAs, and Roth IRAs
- For people age 50 and older, additional "catch-up" contributions are allowed to retirement accounts at work and to IRAs
- A tax credit for low- and middle-income earners who put money into their retirement accounts.

Uncle Sam's new incentives are especially timely in light of the retirement savings setbacks that so many of us suffered in recent years. Now that the catch-up incentives are in place, they offer an opportunity to rethink retirement savings and investments and to benefit from the hard lessons learned during the economic volatility of the last few years. What are these lessons?

- Pay attention to what is happening in your retirement accounts. Read all of your statements; monitor the investments; and once or twice a year, analyze your portfolio carefully and re-balance it if economic conditions are changing.

- Diversify your investments. Experts say that you should not have more than 10 to 15 percent of a retirement account invested in your company stock. You also need to invest in a range of different industries so that if one—such as high technology—drops, you are still reaping benefits from investments in others, such as energy or retail stocks.

- Educate yourself about the various types of retirement savings and investment options—such as individual stocks, mutual funds, and bonds—and the risks of each.

- If you don't feel comfortable managing your retirement savings yourself, seek help from a trusted professional. (See page 40 for tips on how to find one.)

- When you make a financial plan for retirement, consider not only your savings and investments, but all of the building blocks of your financial life—your job and income, your home, and your vision for a retirement lifestyle.

More Americans than ever before are poised to take advantage of the new tax breaks for retirement savings (see page ix for charts). More than a third of households already have some type of IRA, and the number of people with a 401(k) has increased steadily to more than 42 million. Even a nonworking spouse can open an IRA to save for retirement (as long as your income does not exceed certain limits).

The availability of the Internet and the imminent arrival of the baby boomers at retirement age have spawned an explosion

Retirement Savings and Catch-Up Incentives			
Contributions to 401(k), 403(b), and 457 Retirement Accounts		**IRA Contributions**	
Under age 50	**For age 50 and older** (includes "catch-up" contribution)	**Under age 50**	**For age 50 and older** (includes "catch-up" contribution)
2002: $11,000	$12,000	2002: $3,000	$3,500
2003: $12,000	$14,000	2003: $3,000	$3,500
2004: $13,000	$16,000	2004: $3,000	$3,500
2005: $14,000	$18,000	2005: $4,000	$4,500
2006: $15,000	$20,000	2006: $4,000	$5,000
		2007: $4,000	$5,000
		2008: $5,000	$6,000
(After 2006, the regular and catch-up contribution limits will be indexed to inflation and increased in $500 increments. For information on increased limits for other types of pension plans such as a SIMPLE Plan or SEP, consult your financial advisor or the IRS at 1-800-829-1040 or www.irs.gov.)		(After 2008, regular contribution limits will be indexed to inflation and increased in $500 increments; catch-up contribution limits will not increase.)	

Tax Credit for Low- and Moderate-Income Savers

Income limits refer to Adjusted Gross Income. You may receive the credit for a contribution of up to $2,000 to your employer plan (401(k), 403(b), 457, etc.) or to an IRA. For example, an individual who puts $2,000 into an IRA would receive a credit of $1,000 toward payment of federal income tax in that year.

Tax Filing Status	Income	Credit	Maximum Credit
Individual	$0–$15,000	50%	$1,000
Joint	$0–$30,000	50%	$1,000
Individual	$15,001–$16,250	20%	$ 400
Joint	$30,001–$32,500	20%	$ 400
Individual	$16,251–$25,000	10%	$ 200
Joint	$32,501–$50,000	10%	$ 200

of financial interest and activity that would have been impossible to predict as recently as a decade ago. We live in a time and place of unequaled access to information and alternatives for managing our lives and futures. Anyone who really cares about planning and saving for retirement has easy access to tools and advice for everything from figuring out when to go on Social Security, to calculating exactly how much income you'll need when you retire. (You will find many of these tools listed in the "Tips" section at the end of each chapter in this book.)

Despite the hoopla that surrounded the bull market, even before the recent economic decline, many Americans simply were not saving enough for a comfortable retirement. A 1997 study by Public Agenda found that 46 percent of Americans—including people ages fifty-one to sixty-one—had saved less than $10,000 for retirement. More recently, the 2001 "Retirement Confidence Survey" found that a third of all workers had saved less than $10,000 for their retirement. An AARP study of baby boomers reports that the typical boomer had only $1,000 in assets and only one-fifth of boomers had more than $25,000. The rate of personal savings has been spiraling downward from 9 percent of disposable income in 1982 to zero twenty years later.

Most people who have a 401(k) or IRA do not max out their annual contributions, and 20 percent of people who could open a 401(k) have not done so. For the average wage earner who retired in 2001 at the normal retirement age of sixty-five, Social Security replaced only about 38 percent of previous income. Yet financial advisors say most people need about 70 percent of their pre-retirement income to live comfortably in their golden years. (How much of your earnings will be replaced by Social Security in the future depends, of course, on the evolution of the economy and whether the government changes the system for financing the program.)

Clearly there are a lot of Americans who need to catch up on their saving for retirement. In a bygone, simpler era, the strategies available for ensuring financial comfort in retirement were pretty straightforward. If you were lucky, you or your spouse worked for a company or perhaps for a government agency that guaranteed a pension. You knew that when you attained a certain age, after a certain number of years of work, you could count on receiving that pension check on a regular basis. If you didn't have a traditional pension, there was really only one other option: put all of your extra cash into savings accounts, stocks and bonds, or real estate. Although some employees had access to tax-deferred retirement plans in the 1950s, millions of Americans could not benefit from tax incentives to save for retirement until the creation of 401(k)s in 1978 and the extension of eligibility for Individual Retirement Arrangements (IRAs) to all workers in 1981.

And since in the twentieth-century Americans did not live as long as they do now, the need to figure out how to stretch their retirement savings was less compelling than it is now. Now, however, it's clear that in addition to longevity, many factors have combined to make the whole business of saving for retirement more complex: the decline in access to traditional pensions; the shift to IRAs, 401(k)s, and other tax-advantaged retirement vehicles that challenge you to make an almost constant stream of investment decisions; and the intense competition in the financial services industry to manage your retirement funds.

"How do I figure out how much money I'll really need when I retire? Can I count on receiving Social Security? How much risk should I take when I am investing my retirement money? Is it too late for me to save for retirement?"

Many people are so scared by these questions that they put off planning for retirement altogether. After the market volatility of recent years, others who thought they were on track with retirement savings now face the challenge of rebuilding their retirement accounts. At forty, fifty, sixty, or even older, they may suddenly realize that their retirement prospects are grim. They may even think their situations are hopeless. *The Retirement Catch-Up Guide* examines how those of us who haven't planned or prepared adequately **can make up for lost time at any age**—even those of us who are already retired.

That's what I found out when I began to interview people for this book. Since there's no shortage of financial advice available, I thought that rather than give a textbook lesson in financial planning, I would share the real stories of people who have used those strategies and techniques successfully.

The people I interviewed had to play catch-up for a myriad of reasons: bad investments, poor money management, credit card debt, losses in a divorce settlement, a business failure, or just plain low income. When I was searching for examples to write about, one friend said something like this: "What you're looking for is very difficult, because you are requiring people to admit that they have made a mistake, and nobody wants to do that. It's a very negative approach." Yet what I found was quite different: All of these stories are positive because they show that despite the adversity or inattention that stymied the protagonists from saving enough earlier in life, each one has acknowledged the problem and begun to attack it.

What was most surprising, however, was the number of people who appear to be living a solidly middle- or upper-middle-class lifestyle, with expensive cars and capacious homes, vacations overseas, and children in private school, who are very unprepared financially for retirement and have only the most general idea about what they need to do to remedy their situation. Even some people who are quite sophisticated about investing in the stock market have no idea how much Social Security they might receive, let alone how to create what financial planner Duke Grkovic of Richmond, Virginia, calls a "road map" to follow from their current assets to a target they have set for retirement. Yet despite these uncertainties and knowledge gaps, everyone described in this book was consciously taking steps to catch up on saving for retirement—or if they were already retired, had at some time in the past made financial adjustments designed to improve their retirement security. Most of the people whose stories are told here awakened to this need and started to adjust their financial habits when they were in their forties or fifties. But there are also stories about people who may have even been retired for a decade or more, who realized only after they stopped working that they hadn't saved enough to maintain the lifestyle they wanted.

LOOKING FOR LESSONS

Finding the stories that make up the most important part of this volume has been a fascinating odyssey. Once I'd committed to writing the book and started talking about it publicly, many stories came to me simply through word of mouth, friends, or business contacts who were aware of the project. Others I had to actively solicit. The Internet—including bulletin boards and forums for investors, expatriates, and retirees—generated many other stories, including some from Americans living in or planning to live in other countries. In almost every case, I personally interviewed the protagonists of these fifty-four "lessons" in person, by phone, or e-mail. But there were a few instances where professional advisers spoke to me about their clients' experiences, keeping the clients' names and other identifying factors completely anonymous.

In choosing the examples, I did not make a judgment about how much money any individual or family actually requires to catch up on retirement savings, or about what constitutes an acceptable retirement lifestyle. These decisions are truly a matter of personal perspective, so I accepted what people told me about these issues at face value regardless of whether I agree with them. Some of the people in this book will be immensely relieved to be able to count on an annual retirement income of $25,000. Others—some of whom may have $200,000 or more in the bank, plus a pension—believe that they need $1 or $2 million to achieve their goal.

Perhaps the most important lesson is this: Even if you do not have a high enough income to max out contributions to retirement accounts and take full advantage of the new tax laws, you still have many other retirement catch-up options. Despite these apparent differences in people's assumptions about their retirement needs, some themes that helped me to understand the catch-up phenomenon did emerge from studying these lessons:

Many people employ not just one but two or more strategies for catching up on retirement resources. Steve, in chapter 5, emphasizes paying down his mortgage, but he's also committed to driving cars for many years instead of continually investing in new, more expensive vehicles. Jenny, in chapter 3, decided to phase into retirement, but she only did so after employing another strategy—systematically analyzing all of her financial resources and shifting some of them into income-producing investments.

A financial adviser can play an important role in creating a viable retirement catch-up strategy. A certified financial planner, a broker, even a tax lawyer or a CPA—depending on that person's experience—can often help clients who would never do it on their own to set realistic, quantitative goals for retirement savings based on assumptions about longevity, inflation, and growth in investments.

If you need expert help, you should carefully evaluate the adviser you choose before making a long-term commitment. Grace, in chapter 9, admits that she never received a clear explanation of the fees she was paying to a broker who was supposed to be managing her portfolio but who could not seem to stop making errors in her account records. She does know that when she moved the account to a different manager, her costs went down and he was able to explain her options to her in a way that she could understand.

It truly is never too late to catch up on retirement savings. The longer we live, and the longer we expect to live, the more years we have to save, as well as spend, for retirement. Eric and Sheryl in chapter 3 are a good example of this: He is already retired and collecting Social Security, but it's only in the last year or two that he opened an IRA for the first time.

HOW TO USE THIS BOOK

Each chapter of *The Retirement Catch-Up Guide* presents a major strategy for building a secure financial base for retirement. Within each chapter there are three sections: an introduction that describes some of the basic issues raised by the strategy in the title; several true stories that illustrate practical ways that the title strategy can be implemented; and tips to help you get information or otherwise start to follow the example of the lessons described in that chapter.

Every story in *The Retirement Catch-Up Guide* is true. However, all of the names and, in some cases, other facts such as the individuals' jobs or where they live have also been changed to protect their privacy.

Chapter One

Check Up
On All Your
Retirement Resources

Figuring out how to catch up on all the retirement savings you may need for the rest of your life may seem like an insurmountable project. The best way to approach this task, like any other complex task, is to break it into smaller, more manageable steps. If you're writing a book, it's easier to organize and write it by chapters. If you're redecorating your home, break the job down room by room.

To catch up on retirement savings, there are three basic steps:

1. Figure out what retirement resources you have now or can count on.
2. Make a plan that will generate the amount of income and assets you'll need to live on.
3. Implement the plan.

Other chapters in this book address the second and third steps. This chapter is dedicated to ensuring that you have a complete picture of all of the potential assets and income that will be available to you for retirement. Be warned that this exercise can have results that are either pleasing or upsetting. On the negative side, you could find out that your Social Security benefit will be much less than you expected. On the positive side—and this really does happen—you could discover that you've got money in a pension fund you'd forgotten about.

No matter what the numbers tell you, what's importar't is that once you know the facts, you'll be in a position to develop strategies to help you reach your goal.

A RETIREMENT RESOURCES CHECKLIST

When you undertake the inventory of your financial resources for retirement, where should you look? Here are some bases to be sure to touch:

Social Security

More than 99 percent of Americans are eligible to receive some retirement benefit from Social Security. Your benefit is based on a formula that takes into account your thirty-five highest earning years. You receive Social Security credit each year for income up to a specified amount or "wage base." For 2002, that amount is $84,900. In other words, if you earn more than $84,900 you will not get extra credit for Social Security.

Anyone who is twenty-five or older who has done some work covered by Social Security is supposed to automatically receive a four-page "Social Security Statement" three months before his or her birthday each year. Don't throw this statement away! Take the time to look at page 2, where you will see—based on your earnings to date—approximately how much your retirement benefit would be if you retired at age sixty-two, at "full retirement age,"* and at age seventy. If you have not received your free statement or can't find it, order another one from Social Security (see "Tips" at the end of this chapter) and study the information on it carefully.

---

* This is the age when you receive what is generally referred to as your full or normal benefit. That age is sixty-five for people born in 1937 or earlier. For people who were born between 1938 and 1960, full retirement age will be sixty-six. By 2027, full retirement age will be sixty-seven for people born after 1959.

CHART I-A: FULL RETIREMENT AGE, BASED ON YEAR OF BIRTH

YEAR OF BIRTH	FULL RETIREMENT AGE
1937 or earlier	65
1938	65 and 2 months
1939	65 and 4 months
1940	65 and 6 months
1941	65 and 8 months
1942	65 and 10 months
1943–1954	66
1955	66 and 2 months
1956	66 and 4 months
1957	66 and 6 months
1958	66 and 8 months
1959	66 and 10 months
1960 and later	67

These figures can help you estimate how much retirement income you will need from other sources and decide what is the best retirement age for you. And, as you'll see in some of the stories in this chapter, the figures may also spur you to take some steps to increase that benefit—such as asking for a raise or finding a higher-paying job

Also on the Social Security Statement, look at page 3, at the year-by-year listing of how much income has been credited toward your retirement benefit. If you see a year with a zero, or if you see, for example, that in 1985 you were credited with $10,000 and you know you earned $30,000, that means there could be a mistake in your record. It's important to correct such mistakes, because your benefit could be lower if you don't get credit for all of your earnings. If you have your original pay stubs or other documentation of earnings, check them to verify the correct numbers and relay the information to Social Security. For help in doing this, call the Social Security toll-free number at 800-772-1213.

Pensions

Start by making a list of every job you have ever had. The year-by-year record on your Social Security Statement may be helpful in constructing the list.

Then try to remember: Did I receive any retirement benefits from that job? If so, do I know what I must do to collect those benefits? It's amazing how many people actually forget about a pension. One woman in her fifties who had worked as a college teacher decades earlier totally forgot that she had a pension account with TIAA-CREF, the company that provides retirement accounts for employees in academia. She found out about it only when the resident at one of her previous addresses forwarded a statement to her.

Another woman, already retired for about eight years, did not remember that when she taught school forty years earlier in Wisconsin, the county system had put about $600 into a pension account for her. So at age seventy-three she received a letter from a family acquaintance who saw her name on a list of people with "unclaimed accounts" published in the Milwaukee newspaper. The good news is that this retiree had accumulated a $22,000 windfall in that account. The bad news is that she did not have the luxury of investing, managing, or even spending that money during all of those years.

If you think you might have a pension coming to you, contact the employer about it. If you can't find the employer because the company has closed down or has terminated its pension plan, you can search for the pension through a government-chartered agency called the Pension Benefit Guaranty Corporation (PBGC). This agency takes over closing or failing pension plans, distributing the pensions to workers who have earned them. See the "Tips" section for information on how to search for a lost pension through the PBGC system.

Other job-related retirement accounts

The number of Americans who have defined benefit or traditional pensions—which guarantee a certain retirement payment after a certain number of years of work—is declining steadily. In place of the traditional pension, employers have been establishing defined contribution plans such as 401(k)s in the private sector, 403(b)s in the nonprofit sector, and 457s for some public employees. Generally the employer contributes some money to these accounts, matching employee contributions up to a certain percentage, but it's up to the employee to choose the account's investment options and monitor and manage the account.

Up to certain limits, the contributions you make to these accounts are tax-free until you withdraw the money after age fifty-nine and a half. (If you take money out before age fifty-nine and a half, you must pay a 10 percent penalty to the IRS.) When you leave a job where you have a defined contribution plan, you may be required to take the money out of the company account in a lump sum. If you don't "roll over" those funds into an IRA or a similar account with your new employer within sixty days, you'll have to pay a penalty of 10 percent plus income tax on the withdrawal. In some cases, an employer may allow you to leave your money in the account even if you go to another job. If this option will produce a better return than the option at your new job, then you can leave the account with your former employer. Just make sure that you continue to monitor what is happening to that money.

When you compile your list of potential retirement resources, review and document exactly where any of this money from defined contribution accounts might be now, and figure out how much you have in each account. In this category, also be sure to include the money you have in profit-sharing, money purchase, or other types of job-related accounts.

Individual Retirement Accounts

It's not uncommon, especially for people who are relatively young and working on a job with no pension, to find yourself tossing up to $2,000 a year into a different IRA every year or two. The more you do this, the more paperwork you have, the harder it is to track those accounts, and usually, the more administrative fees you are paying to maintain them. Take the time to go through your desk and all your financial documents to make sure you know where all of those IRAs are, and how much money is in them. Also look at how the investments are doing, as a preliminary to developing a comprehensive savings and investment plan for your retirement.

Personal savings

Money that you are saving and/or have invested in accounts outside the tax-qualified retirement accounts listed here can also be an asset for your retirement. Be sure to include the money in savings and brokerage accounts in your inventory.

Inheritances

Without intending to be ghoulish or to get into the complex topic of estate planning, if you know that you will inherit some money or other property of value before you retire, include that on our list. On the other hand, don't be too quick to assume that you'll actually receive a specific amount of money at a specific time. As the average life span increases, Americans are using more of their assets to pay basic living expenses into their late eighties and nineties. Also be aware that probate can delay receipt of an inheritance, and if more than one heir is involved, there is always the possibility of controversy over disposition of an estate.

Real estate

Do you own property that you might sell to produce extra retirement savings? Do you own rental property that produces income now or will produce retirement income in the future? These assets should also go on your retirement resources list.

Business assets

If you are full or part owner of a business, will you be able to continue receiving income from it in retirement, or will you be able to sell your share in return for cash? This too can be a resource that helps pay your living expenses in retirement.

Now What Do I Do?

Once you've identified these assets and potential assets, you can start to develop a budget and a financial plan to reach your retirement goals. The information you've gleaned from searching the eight sources listed here can help you determine how much retirement income you can count on from existing sources—and how much you'll need to make up in other ways, such as by working part-time or increasing your savings.

RETIREMENT RESOURCES CHECKLIST

Social Security	_____	Personal savings	_____
Pensions	_____	Inheritances	_____
Other job-related retirement accounts (401k, 403b, 457)	_____	Real estate	_____
		Business assets	_____
Individual Retirement Accounts	_____		

The stories related in the rest of this chapter will illustrate how taking the time to inventory and determine exactly how much their retirement resources were worth helped motivate a number of real people to start catching up on their retirement savings.

#1

Find Out How Much Your Social Security Retirement Benefit Will Be.

In 2002, the average benefit for an individual is $852. For a couple, it's $1,418. Even though it's usually not enough to pay all the bills, Social Security is the one retirement benefit that virtually every American can count on receiving. It's also probably the only retirement benefit you'll have that is indexed for inflation and will keep up with cost of living increases.

Seeing these dollar figures can be a strong incentive for developing a plan for retirement savings. Because for most people, your Social Security benefit will increase if you make more money, this information might also help you realize that you need to look for a job with higher pay or better benefits, or to do some moonlighting or consulting that will also help increase your retirement stash.

When she was around fifty, Amanda took a hard look at her Social Security record and realized that all she could count on in retirement would be "like a welfare check—maybe about $300 a month." Although she had already taken steps toward retirement security by investing in real estate, the Social Security figures spurred her to redouble her efforts to earn more income.

Amanda's work record was very patchy. By age twenty-five, she was married and the mother of three children. She married and divorced twice and had minimal financial resources after each marriage. She'd worked part-time in a clothing factory, helped run a nursery and landscape design business, and owned an antique shop. While supporting her children and helping them pay for college, Amanda somehow squeezed out the time and money to complete a bachelor's degree and then a master's in counseling psychology, thus attaining the credentials she needed for subsequent jobs as a counselor, therapist, and head of an agency that provided adoption and maternity services.

In 1988, at age forty-five, Amanda recalls, "I had no money in a retirement fund." What she did have was some income-producing real estate. "I've always been interested in real estate," she recalls. "When I was growing up, my parents had a cottage on our property that was always rented out. My mother was in real estate, my father was an architect, and real estate was table talk in our home."

When she was raising her children alone, "for five or six years my mother gave me about $10,000 each year. I spent some of it for my son's education, and also saved some of that." With these savings and an additional $20,000 from her mom, Amanda managed to buy an eleven-acre farm that had a house, a cottage, and a barn on the property. She moved into the house herself and took out loans to improve the other buildings. These investments now add up to a total of seven apartments, a cottage, and office space that she rents out.

"Overall, it's really gone well," says Amanda of her real estate enterprise, but she's "burned out" from managing the property. When times are good and all of the office and apartment units are rented, Amanda grosses about $40,000 a year, but "all of the leases renew from about June 1 to August 1," and this makes her nervous, because "with eight units, every-one could leave at once."

After reviewing the Social Security statement that projected a retirement benefit of around $300, Amanda decided that she should not count on her uncertain real estate income to finance her retirement. She'd saved about $45,000, but "I thought I needed to build up my Social Security," she recalls, so she renewed her license as a substitute teacher and also tried to build up a private mental health counseling practice. Recently, because her private practice was not producing the income she hoped for, Amanda closed it down. Instead, she decided to go back to working at a social service agency where she can count on a certain amount of income—and also on putting away retirement savings on a regular basis.

And not only has she saved money. Amanda's Social Security statement through September 1996 showed that at age sixty-two she could get $345 a month; at age sixty-five, $475, and age seventy-two, $650. A year later the amounts had already gone up significantly—respectively to $475, $725 and $1,080.

#2

If You're Divorced, Check On Whether You Could Get a Higher Social Security Benefit Based on Your Ex's Work Record.

If you were married for at least ten years and are divorced, you may be entitled to a retirement benefit equal to half of the ex-spouse's benefit—if it is larger than your own.

Let's say that you stayed home for several years raising children and then worked part-time for a few years, entitling you to a Social Security benefit of $400 per month. Your ex-spouse has worked full-time at a high-paying job for more than thirty years, and is entitled to a benefit of $1,400 per month. If you can meet the qualifications, once your ex-spouse is at least sixty-two, you could get $700 a month based on the spouse's work record. Your spouse does not have to know that you are receiving the money, and it does not affect the amount the spouse receives.

Ruth is sixty-three. She is a full-time schoolteacher. Before her divorce in 1980, she had no retirement savings. As thoughts of retirement started to loom, she checked with Social Security to see what size retirement benefit she could count on. She was entitled to $698 per month starting at age sixty-two; or $934 per month if she waited until turning sixty-five. She contacted Social Security to see if she might get a higher benefit by collecting based on the work record of her husband, who was a college professor, but it didn't work. Her own benefit equals more than half of her husband's.

Now Ruth's facing a dilemma. She's exhausted from teaching and because she has not spent her entire career in the school system, if she retired now her pension would only be 40 percent of her salary—perhaps less than she really needs to live on. Equally discouraging, if she worked for one more year, she'd get 42 percent. At age sixty-five, she'd receive 44 percent of her salary. But Ruth knows that those amounts are a long way off from the full pension she'd have received if she'd joined the school system earlier in her career.

The income she receives from a small counseling practice on the side barely pays the bills for the extra phone line and other business expenses. One reason is that she's especially interested in helping women who do not have the resources to pay the full cost of their therapy, so she charges them $10 per session instead of the $40 or $50 that is the going rate.

Like many women, Ruth earned her teaching degree early in life but decided to devote most of her time raising two children. Over the years she had some part-time jobs and even got her real estate license. While the children were growing up, "I occasionally sold a property and made some nice money, but I put no money into retirement. I thought my husband was going to take care of me," she explains.

Now Ruth is trying to catch up. She puts $150 per month into a retirement account, and has invested the entire $40,000 inheritance she received when her mother died a couple of years ago. Because it was convenient, she put the inheritance in the hands of a broker who lives in the same city—more than a thousand miles from her own home—where her mother lived. When last interviewed, she was on the verge of having her first detailed discussion with that broker about the best way to invest the inheritance.

#3

List All Your Jobs and Employers and What Retirement Benefits You're Entitled to Receive from Each.

You can't plan for your future unless you have a complete picture of your current resources. For people who need to catch up, this is an essential first step.

When she was about fifty-five, Bethany decided it was time to get some control over the financial side of her life and start planning for retirement. The first step in this process was reviewing all the jobs she'd had, and the benefits she'd earned, in order to make up a realistic plan.

The inventory of retirement benefits from her jobs was pretty depressing. With a degree and a deep interest in art history, Bethany had begun her work life in the museum world. During the seven years she worked for a museum, "they put a tiny amount—about $2,700" into a retirement fund for her, but she did not save it when she left her job. In the following years, she became an expert in technical writing and the editing and design of instructional materials, working for a major university, for a small technology firm, and as a freelancer. None of these jobs produced any retirement savings. Even when she was working for herself, she did not start to save in an IRA.

Her income throughout those years did not allow for luxuries. "The truth is that there were times when I could barely pay my phone bill or my electric bill," she admits. So in addition to not saving for retirement, Bethany ran up debt on credit cards, for a car, and a $20,000 IRS bill.

At age forty-eight, Bethany finally got a job at a technology company with a profit-sharing plan. With sporadic contributions from the employer, this plan has produced about $60,000 in retirement savings for her over the last ten years. More recently, she and other employees convinced the company to start a 401(k), in which she's accumulated about $24,000. But it didn't take long for Bethany to realize that the $84,000 total that she had was definitely not enough to live on in retirement, let alone to pay her bills. Shortly after the company established the 401(k), "I was reading the *Kiplinger's Personal Finance* magazine mutual funds issue," she recalls, "and I realized that in order to retire with 80 percent of my current salary [a percentage often recommended by financial planners], I would need to have $2 million. I know I will never have $2 million," she says, "but my philosophy now is to do as much as possible" to save for retirement.

When Bethany first started making her financial plans for retirement, she expected to work until age seventy, in order to maximize her Social Security and to give the money she would put into the 401(k), a Roth IRA, and some mutual funds as much time as possible to grow. But then, after always being single, she met the man with whom she hopes to spend the rest of her years. Bethany is fifty-eight, but he's six years older and on the verge of retiring. "Since we are planning to spend the rest of our lives together," she explains, it has become more urgent to improve her financial situation. Neither of them owns a house, and they have little furniture between them. "I'd like to have a lifestyle that's comfortable and I realize that $25,000 a year [from Social Security] is just not enough."

The greatest advantage Bethany has is that in the last few

years, her income has increased to between $80,000 and $90,000 per year, depending on commissions. With the aid of a financial adviser, she's created a budget to implement a two-pronged strategy: to pay off her debts and save as much as possible for retirement. Now she makes regular payments on the debts, contributes 10 percent annually to her 401(k) and if there's any money left over she puts it into a fund for buying a house or additional investments.

#4

Conduct a Search for All Your Financial Documents.

Going through drawers and files full of financial papers can be a drag. But if you haven't done it in a few years, make a resolution to do it soon. You may be pleasantly surprised with the results.

Chet, sixty-six, needs all the resources he can find to support himself and his seventy-one-year-old wife. They are both on Social Security, but he does freelance writing and desktop publishing in order to make ends meet. In 1999 his income was under $15,500. His wife earns a little extra money by working as a salesclerk in a retail store.

Chet has had some pretty bad financial luck over the years. For two decades, he worked selling surgical supplies for first one company and then another. When he switched jobs, he transferred his pension to the second company, where it was invested in company stock. The company went broke and that was the end of his pension. "Then the next thing that happened is the bank where my money was deposited went bust," he recalls. "I had loans that I was paying off. The FBI came to me and said: 'Pay up.' I turned over everything I had put up for collateral and lost everything."

Then his health problems started. At fifty-eight, Chet was told by his doctor "that I'd better start enjoying my sunrises because I didn't have many years to go," because of a bad heart. In 1991, however, he received a heart transplant that saved his life.

For the last decade or more, Chet says, "it seemed like I never had enough money," and retirement was not a viable financial option. Because of his health problems, Chet also has some extraordinary expenses—about $12,000 a year for prescription drugs—that Medicare does not pay for. But none of this has depressed Chet's spirits. "Despite the fact that I've failed miserably to provide financially for my old age, life is wonderful and still holds promise," says this sixty-six-year-old, who is currently writing a novel and working on a television documentary.

Recently, evidence of that promise surfaced in a very unexpected way. "About twenty-three years ago I bought some stock in a company called Allied Synergy that went broke, and I totally forgot about it. I don't even know what happened to the stock certificates." One day he received a letter in the mail from a "search outfit" and put it aside, thinking "it was a come-on of some sort. I didn't even think about it for thirty days. Then one day I finally called the 800 number that was in the letter."

To his amazement, the search company informed Chet that his old Allied Synergy stock was now Safeway stock and was worth about $10,000. The windfall will not make a huge difference in his life, but there's no doubt that it will ease the pressure little.

This is the only stock Chet has ever owned. When asked if

he was sorry he hadn't kept track and found it sooner, Chet's answer was "I would have gone totally nuts, with the ups and downs in the stock market . . . especially when it bottomed out." Chet doesn't have regrets about his late discovery of the $10,000. But this story illustrates an important lesson: If you can just take the time to sort through your old, musty financial records, you just might find some buried treasure.

#5

If You're Divorced, or Going to Be, Make Sure You Get Your Share of Pension and Other Retirement Assets.

If you or your spouse earn a pension while you are married, this is considered a "joint asset" of both of you. However, emphasizes the Women's Institute for a Secure Retirement, in order to get your share of a pension you must specifically request it during your divorce settlement. But how you split other assets, in addition to the pension, can also make a difference in your financial status when your retirement.

A divorce lawyer in a major eastern city often represents women who have never worked outside the home, or who have not done so long enough to save much for retirement. In many of these cases, she says, "women have no sense that they are entitled to anything from their husband's retirement assets. The husband is saying: 'I have worked for it and it is mine.' Yet the truth is that the woman has worked in the home, allowing the husband to work on the outside and earn the retirement." She offers this advice to women who are negotiating a divorce settlement: Instead of placing priority on continuing to live in the family home, "go for the retirement assets or the assets you can use for the retirement. Don't insist on keeping the home." Here is the story of a woman who did manage to keep the family home, but also ensured herself a comfortable retirement by getting her share of jointly owned real estate.

Iris, a native of Europe, married an American and came to live in the United States with her husband in 1966. She and her husband both had jobs in education. When he lost his position, she started supplementing their income by baking bread in her kitchen, marketing it through a local shop. As the public clamored for the bread, the business grew and she and her husband worked in it together. As it turned out, neither the personal nor the business partnership succeeded on a long-term basis. When working together became difficult, Iris got a real estate license and the family began buying apartment buildings.

A couple of years later, in 1985, when she was forty-seven years old, she was divorced and became "the sole support of three children and our house." While they were married, this couple did not save for retirement. The only retirement income that Iris could count on was going to be from Social Security, which she'd been paying into as a self-employed businesswoman. But one thing she and her husband had was real estate. "We had bought some apartment buildings along the way," she explains, "and I ended up with two of those." While she and her husband were in the divorce process, she bought a third apartment building from him. They'd acquired this property for $13,000 in 1968; she paid $92,000 for it in 1985, "and now it's worth $130,000," Iris says.

While her children were still at home, Iris lived frugally, using the apartment rents to upgrade the buildings and taking advantage of the tax deductions. She also worked as a real estate agent, and "whenever I received a commission from selling something, I put it away in mutual funds."

"I was always afraid I wouldn't have enough money," Iris says. The day came when she started considering retirement and went to a friend who's a broker for advice. To her surprise, at age sixty-one, she learned that she could afford to retire and live comfortably.

The stock market had treated Iris well. Her mutual funds had grown to a value of more than $300,000, and, of course, the rents were flowing in every month from the eleven apartments. The mortgage on her own home is covered by the income from one apartment building. Adding about $10,000 a year from her investment capital, even without collecting Social Security of about $800 a month, Iris has positioned herself to fully enjoy her retirement years. And what is it that she wants to do? She ticks off some of her activities: "I go on trips for Elderhostel. I have relatives I visit in Europe; later in the year I will go to the south of France for a twelve-day cooking class." Iris adds that when she's at home there are the regularly scheduled tennis games with her friend the broker.

Iris can thank her divorce lawyer for the nice life she is leading now. It's not that she hasn't worked hard. But without her share of the real estate from her marriage, she might still be baking bread in her kitchen and contemplating a much more constricted retirement life based only on her income from Social Security.

#6

If You Think You've "Lost" a Pension, Search for It Through the Pension Benefit Guaranty Corporation (PBGC).

To prevent employees from losing a pension that they have earned, the government created an agency to take over pension plans that are closing down for a variety of reasons—for example, because the company goes out of business, or is bought by another company, or is bankrupt. When last contacted, this agency had the names of about 10,000 people whose pensions they were prepared to distribute—if the agency could only find them! If you suspect that your name could be on the list, be sure to check the website at http://search.pbgc.gov, or contact the agency through the address listed in the "Tips" section of this chapter.

Diane is sixty-four now, and she's been retired on disability for about seven years. She's worked since she was eighteen years old, as a bookkeeper and in other office positions for several companies and a state agency. But she's also had serious health problems for a number of years. After Diane had a heart attack, her doctor told her she simply was not healthy enough to work any longer.

Despite her long years of work, when Diane retired in

1992 she had no pensions or other retirement accounts. Her husband had died and left her without financial resources. Getting along financially was a difficult challenge, because it took her about two years—and a battle involving a lawyer and her congressman's office—to get approval to receive her Social Security disability payments.

While she was waiting for approval of her Social Security benefit, one day her son was surfing on the Internet and came across the website for the PBGC. He looked up Diane's name and found it on the agency's list of people who were owed pensions by a medical supply company where she had been employed for three and a half years.

"My son called me up and said the government had some money for me. I called and they said it was true. I had to provide some identification, and a marriage certificate because my name had changed." When the formalities were complete, Diane received $15,000, of which more than $3,000 had to be paid out in income tax. Unfortunately, she couldn't afford to invest or save the money. "I used the money right away," to cover immediate expenses, she recalls, "because I was still waiting to get my Social Security. I had a son who was still in college and I helped him. The only thing I bought for myself was a washer and dryer." But, without that windfall of $12,000, Diane would have been in an even worse financial situation.

7

Check Up On Your IRAs and Consider Consolidating Them.

Every year around the end of March, newspaper, magazine, and even television advertisements urge you to buy an Individual Retirement Account before the April 15 tax deadline. Every working person and nonworking spouse (within certain income limits) has the right to a tax deduction of up to $3,000 per year for money deposited in an IRA. If you are 50 or older, you may contribute up to $3,500 in 2002 through 2004, and higher amounts in later years. (See chart on page ix.) For this purpose, the "year" is defined as any time up until the April 15 tax deadline. This means that the money you spend for an IRA, say, on April 10, 2002, will count as a contribution for 2001.

It's easy to forget about or put off contributing to an IRA until the last minute. And at that point, the simplest thing to do may be to walk into your local bank or call up your broker and simply buy whatever was advertised. If you don't pay attention, you could end up with a bunch of IRAs in different accounts, not necessarily invested as well as they could be—and you could also be paying excessive fees. That's exactly what happened to this lawyer, who should have known better.

Aren't all lawyers rich? And don't they all follow the most reliable advice about how to invest and save for retirement? In this case, a lawyer who specializes in divorce and other domestic issues admits rather sheepishly to some lapses in his own financial arrangements.

Lee has a terrific record of helping people come out on top in their divorce settlements. He's a good negotiator and is very clever about making sure his clients come out of a marriage with as much money and property as possible. For many years Lee has worked in law firms that did not have pension plans. "The only way I can get a tax break to save for retirement is an IRA," he says, and he knows that those savings alone are not enough. "People whose tax-qualified retirement savings are limited to an IRA should also set up a brokerage account to use as a savings vehicle for the future."

That said, Lee has contributed some money to IRAs during his career, but it's only recently that he began putting in the full $2,000 per year. Now, at age forty-eight, he has focused on the fact that he'd been saving for retirement in four different IRAs and paying $240 in annual management fees— $60 to each one. "That's not a lot of money," he says, "but I'd rather have it in my pocket."

Currently Lee is evaluating the investments in each of his IRAs so that he can make the best decision about consolidating the accounts. When he's finished this task, he'll have done himself two favors: reduced the annual IRA management fees, and because the investments will not be so dispersed, probably get better returns on his money.

TIPS

 Get an up-to-date estimate of your potential Social Security retirement benefit. Everyone age twenty-five and over who has worked in a job covered by Social Security is supposed to get a copy of his or her Social Security Statement three months before each birthday. The estimates on these automatic statements are based on your earnings to date. If you expect your income to change between now and retirement, you can order a statement based on your anticipated future income or use the "calculators" in the "Retirement Planner" on the Social Security Administration's (SSA) website, www.ssa.gov.

To get a statement, either call the SSA's toll-free line, 800-772-1213, or request it through the website.

 If you cannot locate a previous employer and you think you've "lost" a pension, contact the Pension Benefit Guaranty Corporation, a government-chartered agency in Washington, D.C., for help. You can actually search for the pension under your own name through the website at www.pbgc.gov. Or you can request help by writing to the PBGC at 1200 K St. N.W., Suite 240, Washington, DC 20005-4026, or by calling them at 202-326-4000.

 Learn the rules of how the different types of IRAs work—how much you can contribute, income limits, and tax implications. Although the language can be dense, the most authoritative source is IRS Publication 590, "Individual Retirement Arrangements (IRAs)." You can order a copy by calling the IRS's toll-free publications line, 800-829-3676, or through the agency's website, www.irs.ustreas.gov.

If you are involved in a divorce, inform yourself about your rights so that you can protect your share of joint assets from the marriage. Here are some resources that can help you:

- The website of the Women's Institute for a Secure Retirement (WISER), at http://www.wiser.heinz.org. Look for the general section on divorce, and within it, the fact sheet "Pensions & Divorce."

- Send $3.00 to WISER for their booklet "What Every Woman Needs to Know About Money and Retirement," at 1920 N Street, N.W., Suite 300, Washington, D.C. 20036.

- Two free publications—"Women and Pensions: What Women Need to Know and Do" and "QDRO's: The Division of Pensions Through Qualified Domestic Relations Orders"—can be ordered through the U.S. Department of Labor's publications hotline: 800-998-7542.

CHAPTER TWO

MAKE A PLAN

> "Developing a financial plan is the most effective way to achieve saving goals."
>
> —*Stephen Brobeck,*
> *Executive Director, Consumer Federation of America*

Are you a financial planner? You don't have to earn a professional degree and have an acronym after your name to be a financial planner. All you have to do to qualify is consciously carve out some time to analyze your own financial situation, project your future needs, and devise realistic financial strategies to make sure you will be able to meet those needs.

The 2000 Retirement Confidence Survey, sponsored by the Employee Benefit Research Institute, the American Savings Education Council, and Matthew Greenwald and Associates, dubbed 27 percent of one thousand respondents as "planners." The majority of these planners reported that they:

- Are disciplined savers;
- Always research and plan for big purchases;
- Enjoy financial planning; and
- Believe that they will have enough money to cover basic expenses in retirement, including their medical needs.

Whether these people who call themselves planners are accurate in their optimistic predictions remains to be seen. But assuming they are, that still leaves a little less than three-quarters of American workers as nonplanners. What can they do?

To many people, planning for an unknown future is a contradiction in terms. How can you plan for the future in a fast-changing economy when you don't know what your job will be five years from now? To add to the dilemma, until recently, there has been little in our culture to encourage—let alone enable—most of us to create and stick to a lifelong plan that will guarantee a comfortable retirement. Few, if any, people in the retirement catch-up generation learned the basics of financial planning in school. These lessons simply have not been part of the curriculum. Most of us also didn't learn much about money management from our parents. In many families, money issues are a taboo subject. Children are not supposed to inquire and parents are usually not disposed to talk about family income, what it costs to pay the bills, or how much they've saved in retirement accounts.

The first step toward a comfortable retirement is defining what that means to you. What sort of lifestyle do you want to maintain? Do you want to continue working as long as possible or do you dream of retiring early? Will you want to travel? To be near family? To stay in your current home? Once you begin to answer these questions, you can begin working toward implementing the answers.

The following stories illustrate ways that you can begin. Each story in this chapter describes steps actually taken by real people who postponed creating a retirement plan until the middle or end of their career, and have rebounded to take control of their future by developing plans later in life.

8

Give Your Future a Reality Check.

It's not unusual for people to harbor subconscious assumptions about their retirement life. Even in the twenty-first century, for many women, this takes the form of the unspoken belief that at some point they will meet and marry the perfect provider who will take care of their economic needs for the rest of their life. Of course, the older we get, the less likely it is that this will happen. And so, at some point, it's also not unusual for women who think this way to realize that they must in fact provide their own financial resources for retirement. Here's the story of one woman who confronted that reality at age forty-one.

For nearly two decades, Rita led an incredibly exotic and adventurous life. She lived or traveled extensively in Latin America, becoming fluent in Spanish and indulging a strong personal interest in handicrafts and folk art. What started as an avocation became a business. Until recently, she was selling a million dollars a year worth of imported goods, employing more than sixty people and attending a seemingly endless round of trade shows where she could connect with buyers.

Before starting the business, she'd worked for a foundation and a civil rights organization. In those years, she recalls, "I didn't care at all about saving money or banking and stocks.

For most of my life my priorities have had to do with education, travel, and professional growth and development. Money was probably the lowest priority when I was considering any action or job."

On one overseas business trip, Rita found herself dining with an American stockbroker. The conversation turned to money, and he emphatically told her, "I'm so tired of hearing smart people tell me that they have nothing to retire on. They are stupid and deserve anything they get." Rita, who at this time had neither retirement plans nor savings, asked: "What do you mean?" The stockbroker's reply was to the point: "You put money into an account. There is something called compound interest. If you leave the money in the account, then twenty years later you will have money to retire on."

Rita remembered this conversation, even as she continued to reinvest all the company's returns back in the business. Then, at age forty-one, she had her "fortieth-birthday crisis." "I was taking stock of my life. I realized that all along I had the fantasy that I would marry a professional man, that he would have a good salary and we would have a house and family. Suddenly it became clear that at forty-one, there were no options for marriage in sight. I realized I was all alone in the world. I had to make my own choices."

Soon after that, Rita bought a house and consulted with a stockbroker about how to save for retirement. "We assumed that my house would be paid off. I would drive a very modest car. I'd like to go to Europe once a year for a month. I thought that with $30,000 a year I could live happily ever after." The broker said that she'd need to put away $500 per month to achieve that goal. This seemed like more than she could afford, but interest rates declined, she refinanced her house, and Rita decided to have the $300 per month she was saving on the mortgage deposited in her brokerage account automatically.

Even though she's decided to close down her business and start another career at age fifty-two, Rita feels good about her future. "My anxiety is tremendously reduced knowing that I am doing this," she says. "Had I understood the principle of compound interest earlier, I would not have waited to save until after I was forty years old. I would have started saving from the beginning. If I'd done that, I would have incredible freedom now because my financial worries would have been taken care of."

#9

Create a Retirement Vision.

The more abstract your concept of retirement is, the harder it will be to save and plan to make it a reality. So, even if you know there are likely to be changes en route, a good first step toward taking control of your retirement finances is to visualize how you will live your "new" life. This provides a goal against which you can measure your progress.

Chris and Elliott met at the phone company where they both worked. When they decided in 1995 to get married, at the respective ages of fifty-one and fifty-three, little did they know that the ceremony would lead not only to a marriage but also to a commitment to spend their golden years south of the border.

It all started because they had six children between them, and getting them all together in one place for a wedding was difficult. So they decided to say their vows at a resort near Puerto Vallarta, Mexico. A couple of months before the wedding, Chris recalls, "I came across the address of a Mexican waiter I had become friends with on a previous trip and with whose wife I had corresponded. I had never met her in person, but I dropped her a note and asked if they'd like to come by. Long story short, their whole extended family showed up at the hotel, our friendship blossomed, they stood up with us at the wedding, and put on a traditional Mexican family wedding dinner for us."

Since that happy event, Chris and Elliott have returned to Mexico each year. Each time, this couple from the northeastern United States says, they make more friends and feel more certain that Mexico is where they want to retire. The vision they're holding out for is an affordable home in Nayarit, on the Pacific coast, where they will have access to their new friends and not feel they're living in a "community of gringos." They keep the vision alive by making annual visits, to "a circle of friends that has grown from the original family to many other employees of the resort and their families." Describing her feeling for their future home by e-mail, Chris wrote: "It's a good thing that computers have delete keys, because I'm sure having trouble finding the words for the feeling one gets to be greeted after a year's absence with hugs and tears by people . . . who open up their lives to us as if we're family . . . 'Mi casa es tu casa'—'My home is your home'—is the reality there."

So, during these years, the challenge is to manipulate their budget to finance the vision. Hearing Chris describe the plan—she actually calls it an obsession—one somehow thinks that they, in fact, will figure it out.

#10

Create a Retirement Budget to Support the Vision.

The 2000 Retirement Confidence Study found that almost half of the workers surveyed had not even taken one of the most basic financial planning steps—trying to calculate how much money they need to save by the time they retire. Yet, as Steve Brobeck of the Consumer Federation of America suggests, the mere act of planning has the effect of increasing the savings of people who take the time to do it.

Even if you're not comfortable with numbers, this is not a difficult task. In recent years, the government, employers, and the financial industry have developed and promulgated an array of new, user-friendly tools such as computerized retirement calculators that you can employ to start making your own retirement financial plan. The "Tips" section at the end of the chapter lists some you can start with.

"We had a very simple lifestyle, and we don't care to keep up with the Joneses," declares Darlene. So until five years ago she, now fifty-eight, and her husband, Harold, who is fifty, never focused on saving for retirement or the financial challenges it would present.

Darlene has worked for thirty-eight years "as an underpaid

secretary, the last twenty-two in the defense industry, for two companies." When she was single "I was only able to invest a small amount yearly," she says. Her husband preferred to be his own boss rather than work for other people, so he started using the degrees he'd earned in languages to teach Spanish and Portuguese at a community college and then to give private classes and tutoring.

Late in her career she attended college and took several courses in personal finance, and "these classes made us look at what we had and how we could better utilize it for our future." As a result, they took several financial steps toward creating a retirement budget they could live on and—as this book was being written—actually retiring at ages fifty-eight and fifty.

"At first we decided that I would work until the house was paid for." When interest rates dropped, they refinanced the house, taking out a fifteen-year mortgage to replace the thirty-year mortgage they had before. Then, using funds from a small family inheritance, Darlene and Harold upgraded the property by installing a sprinkler system, hardwood floors, and making other cosmetic changes. Their efforts were repaid. They sold the house for an entirely tax-free $50,000 profit because they lived in Texas. They put the proceeds into an interest-bearing account that will produce an income of about $700 per month—a cornerstone of their retirement budget.

With retirement in mind, over a few years Darlene and Harold searched for an economical place to live in the United States. They ruled out northeast Texas as too hot and humid, and Chicago as too cold. When someone suggested they check out Mexico, they made a visit and seriously started to think about moving there. After four trips, they chose a Mexican town near Guadalajara as their future retirement home. In addition to the cost of housing, food and transportation, Darlene and Harold were concerned about health insurance because they will not be eligible for Medicare until they're sixty-five. (At that point, they would have to return to the

United States to be covered.) They could have secured eighteen months of coverage through Darlene's company plan, but it would have cost them $707 per month. After comparison shopping, they chose a policy with a high deductible—$4,500—but the premium is only $300 a month.

As Darlene and Harold researched the cost of living in Mexico, they also reorganized their retirement resources to maximize their potential income. By consolidating the money in their retirement and savings accounts into two mutual funds, they'll generate about $2,500 a year. Darlene also receives about $3,500 a year from pensions from her current and previous jobs.

Added to the $700 a month generated by the profit on the house, this income provides them about $1,200 a month, which is all they need to rent a home, take taxis for transportation, and generally bask in the warm but not humid climate.

#11

Take Stock of Your Current Income and Resources.

Getting a realistic, complete picture of your finances is a key step in planning for retirement. In this case, the word *finances* encompasses all of your assets, including lump-sum payments, real estate, an inheritance, or alimony. This is a story about a divorced woman who has parlayed the assets she received from her divorce into a retirement nest egg.

Erma is the mother of four adult children. She's been married and divorced four times. Now the editor of an academic journal, she for many years worked in part-time writing and editing jobs that provided little or nothing in the way of retirement savings.

Seven years ago, when she was fifty, Erma received a divorce settlement that, if well managed, will be her ticket to retirement security: a lump sum of $250,000 and seven years of alimony of $38,000. Her first decision was to spend $185,000 of the cash to buy a condo where she can live rent- and mortgage-free through her retirement; she invested the rest.

"When I was fifty-five, I first began to focus on retirement. I really hadn't thought about it before." She went to a financial adviser, who helped her understand how to make the most of the assets she had.

Part of Erma's strategy is what she calls "living minimally. I own my car—a 1992 station wagon—and I plan to keep it as long as I can. I'm not buying big items. I'd like to have all new furniture, but I make choices about what I spend. I subscribe to the ballet and to a summer dance festival, but I don't buy a lot of new clothes."

The seven years of alimony have helped Erma survive while she figures out how to ensure her financial future. In her new job, she'll earn up to $60,000 a year, but she plans to live on the alimony as long it lasts, and save the money from her salary. Erma calculates that when and if she becomes too old to work full-time, she'll have about $500,000 to live on.

And it's a good thing, because a few years ago when she requested an estimate of how much her Social Security retirement benefit would be, the results were pretty depressing: $33.13 per month.

#12

Plan for a Long, Productive Life.

If your relatives tend to live a long time, you need to consider that in your own retirement planning. That means that at age fifty or even sixty, you need to think not just about quitting work, but about what you're going to do for another thirty or forty years.

Tillie's mom is eighty. Her dad is eighty-two, and her grandmother lived until age ninety-four. That's why she says: "I intend to live a long time." Tillie is fifty-five and she's eager to plan the rest of her life. After earning a master's degree in statistics, for seventeen years she worked in government agencies, accumulating some money in a pension fund. But at the same time she left government work, she got a divorce, and the $45,000 that was supposed to be saved for retirement was spent instead on things like buying a car, paying off bills, and putting a down payment on a condo.

In her fifties, Tillie went to work for a private company, where she started having 6 percent of her paycheck put into a 401(k), which the employer company matched with 1 percent of her salary. She also acquired stock options. Around the same time, Tillie also enrolled in a Ph.D. program in a high-tech field, spending about $40,000 to get her degree recently. "It cost almost $40,000 of my retirement savings, but I did it because I expect to have increased income in the near term and the potential of earning more as a consultant in the future."

About a year ago she switched jobs, moving to another private employer to gain experience she believes will boost her earnings potential considerably in the next few years.

With the job change, Tillie's been focusing a lot on planning for retirement, and she's putting 10 percent of her salary into the 401(k). Currently there's about $400,000 in the fund, "but I think I'm going to have to work at least ten more years," she says.

Then Tillie will start yet another job: running a bed-and-breakfast. She'll buy a house—probably outside a major city such as New York or Washington, D.C., where she can live, "have at least part of my expenses paid for, meet some interesting people," and maybe even do some consulting on the side.

At the moment she's frustrated, though, because "the financial adviser I'm working with seems to be dragging things out." Although Tillie has a general idea of how she'll spend the next thirty years or so, she's eager to get a precise financial prescription that she can follow. If this adviser doesn't help her do that soon, she says, she'll be looking somewhere else for help.

#13

Shift Gears If Your Original Plans Are Not Panning Out.

The path to achieving your retirement goals is not always a direct one. Jobs may change, investments may earn less than you expect, or you may make mistakes along the way. What's important is to remain flexible so you can adjust to new circumstances.

Michelle, fifty-one, has worked in the field of human resources for twenty-five years, sometimes for a company and sometimes as the owner of her own consulting business. Her husband, Keith, who's fifty-four, was an academic years ago but has been an administrator of a city agency for nearly a decade. They think that they're on track now to attain their goal of early retirement in 2003, but only after having to adjust their financial activities several times.

In the early years of their marriage, when their two children were young, "we lived hand to mouth," Michelle says. "We had absolutely no savings." At one point, they decided to invest in universal life insurance policies for each of them, paying in $26,000 a year. After a few years they consulted a financial planner, who showed them that "you really need about twenty years to build up any kind of funds in the policies," as Michelle says. They cashed out the policies, losing about $10,000, and put the money into other investments.

When Michelle worked for a company, she was earning a

good salary and putting about $600 per month into a 401(k) and profit-sharing plan. Her husband also started a retirement account, saving the same amount each month. But when she started a consulting business and incurred substantial debts, this created another diversion from saving for retirement. To pay off the debt from the business, for two years Michelle did not take a salary, and did not contribute any money to retirement savings. To make matters worse, the investments in her and Keith's retirement accounts did not do well. "They did not hit. We simply were not in the right funds," she says. She began to educate herself about investing, attending seminars and starting to put money into some individual stocks. But overall, her choices have performed below the average of the bull market of the late 1990s.

Despite these setbacks, Michelle and Keith still think they can retire even before he becomes eligible for his $24,000-a-year pension in 2008. In 1998 "I came up with my own plan. I call it Life Plan 2000," she explains. The plan is based on several components: Michelle will start taking a salary from her consulting business again. She will sell an investment property that she's been renting out, and re-invest the proceeds—hopefully at a 15 percent rate of return per year. Another asset that figures in this couple's plan is their home, now worth about $300,000, in which they have nearly $250,000 in equity. Their property consists of twenty-eight acres as well as the house, and they plan to subdivide and sell part of the property for around $50,000, which will also provide more money to invest.

Will they have enough to retire on in a few years? At this point it's impossible to predict. Keith will get a pension of $24,000, but not until he's sixty-two. And at the same age, they'll each be eligible for around $1,200 per month from Social Security. Whether they can retire earlier will depend a lot on their investment returns. But even if Plan 2000 doesn't work out, it's clear that with the resilience they have already demonstrated, Michelle and Keith will be able to devise another plan with another target year. After all, at fifty-one and fifty-four, they are still able to continue working for quite a few years if it's necessary.

#14

Get Help from an Expert You Trust.

If you don't feel confident about doing retirement planning based on your own research and reading, search for a financial adviser you can trust. Before choosing, check out references, and be clear about the services you need and the fees you will have to pay for them.

A financial adviser may be a CPA, a broker, a financial planner, even a tax or estate lawyer. The Better Business Bureau points out that various types of advisers are subject to different "codes of ethics, honesty, and conflicts of interest" which they are obligated to uphold.

If you're considering hiring a financial planner, be sure to ask about how that person is paid. Some planners are "fee-only," meaning that they will charge you a flat or hourly fee for offering advice and helping you develop a plan. Others may charge a commission for selling you investments. Some may charge a combination of a fee and commissions. For leads on how to find an adviser you trust, see the "Tips" section at the end of this chapter.

Rose made a conscious decision not to think about saving for retirement until she was forty years old. "I figured I'd retire when I was sixty-five, and twenty-five years would be plenty of time to save."

When she was forty, Rose was working in an interesting and rewarding job for a nonprofit organization that had a retirement plan. Her employer put 6 percent of her salary into the plan each month but, Rose admits, "I had forgotten my promise to myself. I did not put in any of my own money." After three and a half years, when she was changing jobs, "I realized I really needed to start paying attention. There was about $9,000 in the account. I rolled it over into an IRA."

At that point, her husband had about $60,000 in a retirement account but did not have a systematic savings program. They decided it was time to consult an expert. "We had a healthy financial life, but we had no idea how much we'd need for retirement. We were living in a vacuum," Rose says. They chose a planner who was highly recommended by three people they knew, and they were not disappointed. One of the things they most appreciated was that "he did more than just advise us on investments. He worked with us on our attitudes about money, and he made us realize that how you use money is your decision about what you want to do with your life.

"When we met for the first time, he asked us a bunch of questions and asked us to give him tons of stuff—every financial thing we had." Based on that information and on further conversations, the planner produced what Rose calls "a voluminous thing"—a thick white loose-leaf notebook with color tabs. The book lays out basic planning principles, and contains tables that show exactly how their money will grow, year by year, if they contribute a certain amount each year until they retire.

The planner helped them set some parameters for figuring out how much they need to save: They would aim for a retirement income of 70 percent of their working salary, assume earned interest of 10 percent per year on their investments, and an annual inflation rate of 2 to 3 percent, and that they would each live to be ninety years old.

Together, Rose and her husband are now catching up by contributing nearly $20,000 per year to their retirement plans. It's a lot of money to save, but she says, "I feel fabulous. We are right on the mark and we know exactly how much money we should have at the end of each year." They also know that if they stick to their plan, when they stop working at relatively early ages—she at sixty-two and he at fifty-eight—they will have about $1.4 million to support whatever travel or other activities they want to enjoy in retirement.

TIPS

 Take advantage of all the information and assistance offered by your employer. Many companies offer seminars or even individual counseling in planning, saving, and investments. If you don't know what's available, check with your human resources department. If the company provides software to help you with your own planning, take the time to use it.

 Use Internet resources. These sites can help you start planning. Their interactive programs allow you to plug in your own financial data to find out exactly how big your nest egg will be for retirement, based on your age and assumptions about future earnings, savings, and investment results. These sites are listed in order of complexity. The first on the list requires you to put in the smallest amount of financial information; the last one requires the most detail.

- www.usatoday.com/money.

- www.asec.org. Click on the "Ballpark Estimate."

- http://money.cnn.com/retirement.

- www.quicken.com/retirement.

Check these sites for basic information on retirement planning. They can help you take stock of all of your financial resources, including pensions, IRAs, savings, and 401(k)s.

- www.asec.org. Click on "Savings Tools."

- www./kiplinger.com. Several calculators to help you figure out how much money you'll lose if you borrow from your 401(k).

- www.quicken.com. Information on planning, IRAs, annuities, etc.

 Enlist the help of a good financial planner. Here are some tips on locating and checking out a financial adviser. In addition to asking for referrals from friends, family, colleagues, or other professionals, such as your lawyer, check with these organizations:

- The local Better Business Bureau, or at their website (www.bbb.org), for a one-page summary, "Tips for Consumers: Selecting a Financial Planner."

- Certified Financial Planner Board of Standards. Call 888-237-6275 to order a copy of a helpful thirteen-page brochure, "What You Should Know About Financial Planning"; or go to www.CFP-Board.org and click on "consumers" to get advice on choosing and working with a planner.

- The Financial Planning Association. Call 800-322-4237 or go to www.fpanet.org for information about how to select a financial planner.

- National Association of Personal Financial Advisers, whose members charge fees for planning but do not receive commissions for selling financial products to you. Call 888-333-6659 or go to www.napfa.org.

CHAPTER THREE

READJUST YOUR WORKING PLANS

For most people, a job is the primary factor in determining their level of financial comfort and independence in retirement. Yet, this relationship between job and retirement is even more complex than most of us realize. How much money are you earning, spending, and saving? Does your job provide enough income to save adequately for retirement? Will your job provide a pension or health benefits when you retire? If you take early retirement, will you lose out on some retirement benefits? The answers to these questions depend on job decisions that you may have made a decade or even two or three decades ago.

You cannot change past decisions; you must live with them. But when the moment of retirement planning truth arrives, keep in mind that you do still have some decisions to make and some options from which to choose. Instead of sticking to the same path you've always followed—keeping the same job, retiring at the age you chose twenty years ago, and resigning yourself to a low-budget retirement, don't be afraid to consider other changes in your work life that might enhance your retirement years.

The first option is probably the easiest, especially if your work produces a good salary and benefits: Simply delay your retirement date so that pension or other savings will have more time to grow. The other options for adjusting your work life require more aggressive, perhaps even risky, action.

Consider a new job or career as a catch-up strategy. There are two main reasons for making such major changes:

1. To increase your pre-retirement earnings and, therefore, your retirement savings; and
2. To enhance your ability to work and to earn income, at least part-time, after you start taking Social Security or your pension.

INCREASING PRE-RETIREMENT EARNINGS

Some people have lagging retirement savings because they spend their disposable income on other things—cars, vacations, a bigger house than they really need. For others, the primary barrier to building up retirement savings is truly low income—earnings that barely cover daily expenses, leaving nothing for savings. A lot of factors can result in low income: lack of education or other credentials, working in a low-paying sector of the economy, lack of self-confidence to fight for a raise or a promotion, or working in a small business that does not offer a pension plan or retirement account. If you operate a struggling small business, you might feel that creating a retirement plan for yourself and your employees would be prohibitively expensive.

Even if forced to live on a very constricted budget, you may love your current job and want to stay with it. An academic who is a dedicated teacher may have a lower salary and puny retirement benefits, but may treasure the intangible rewards of teaching. The pastry chef in a fine but small restaurant in the countryside may think she's got her dream job, even though there's no 401(k) plan. And the fifty-year-old computer programmer may luxuriate in having the freedom to set his own work schedule. But, as the examples throughout this book demonstrate, somewhere between the ages of about forty and fifty-five, many people realize for the first time in their work life that unless they take some conscious, even difficult steps to catch up, the resources they'll have when they retire will fall far short of supporting the lifestyle they want.

Whether you've simply not given priority to saving for retirement, or whether you truly have not been earning enough to save, the challenge is the same: to increase your earnings, and dedicate some or all of the increase to savings, in time to build a retirement nest egg.

A first step to catching up may be to ask for a raise or to seek a promotion at your current job. If this is not an option, then the only alternative may be to change your job or career. For someone who has devoted twenty or thirty years to one employer or to working in one field, the prospect of a change so late in life can be daunting. One way to build up the confidence to embark on this path is suggested by Maryellen Gor and Linda Kunder, in their book *Blooming Late: Cultivating Your Self-Esteem After Fifty*. To jump-start your search, try looking back over your entire life and identifying the personal accomplishments on which you can build your future. As you contemplate your life, one decade at a time, and tally those accomplishments, you'll begin to realize that you do have the wherewithal, the talent, the skills, to successfully take on a new challenge in your work life. After all, in your first ten years you learned how to walk and talk and read; in your teens you learned to drive a car, got your high school diploma, learned teamwork by playing basketball, and earned twenty merit badges as a Scout. By now you may have earned a college degree, received a series of promotions into jobs that gave you increasing responsibility, successfully raised children, learned to use a computer or play the piano, and developed a network of colleagues you can consult with on professional issues. In other words, if you have been able to accomplish all of these

things, you should also be able to navigate the waters of a job
or career change that will position you financially for the
lifestyle that you want to have when you retire.

PREPARING FOR A POST-RETIREMENT JOB

Working after retirement? That may sound like a crazy idea,
one that is contradictory to the concept of retirement. Yet, evidence is mounting that an increasing number of Americans
intend to do just that. In a report for the Employee Benefit
Research Institute, Joseph Quinn of Boston College observes
that the post–World War II trend toward men leaving the
labor force at a younger age appears to have "come to an
abrupt halt" in the mid-1980s. In the mid-1990s, Quinn reports, about 28 percent of men and 18 percent of women age
sixty-five to sixty-nine were still working.

A number of factors suggest that as baby boomers reach
what used to be called retirement age, the percentage who are
working at least part-time after they reach sixty-five will increase. *Boomers Approaching Midlife*, a report by the American
Association of Retired Persons (AARP) Public Policy Institute, showed that more than three-quarters of baby boomers
expect to "retire" by age sixty-five, but that close to three-
quarters of those also expect to continue working "at least on
a part-time basis." One important reason for this longer work
life is financial: The same AARP report suggests that although
they will have some other pension and investment income,
"about half of boomers will still depend on Social Security for
half or more of their income." For retirees in this situation,
that's both good news and bad. They will have some income,
but Social Security was never intended to provide enough
money for a truly comfortable and secure retirement. After all,
in December 1998, the average monthly Social Security retirement benefit was $857 for men and $643 for women.

Some retirees, of course, work for reasons that are not financial—to keep busy, to expand their education, to provide service to their community, to maintain professional and social relationships. But this book is about catching up—about compensating for years of inadequate income and/or savings by continuing paid employment beyond sixty-two, when you can start collecting Social Security, or beyond sixty-five, which for decades has been considered the normal retirement age.

If you feel that Social Security and your other savings or pensions will not be enough to support you comfortably in retirement, the time to start thinking about a post-retirement career is now. One thing you can do is to look for a job with an employer who will allow you to work as long as you want and offers better benefits than you receive now. Another approach is to take a *bridge job* or opt for *phased retirement*. These terms can mean anything from working three-quarters or half-time, to converting your position to a consultant or temporary status, taking on seasonal work or even finding a colleague with whom you can share a job. Although it is still hard to find companies or organizations with structured phased retirement programs, the prospects for negotiating these types of work arrangements seem to be on the rise. In a recent survey of nearly 600 employers with 3.2 million employees, the employee benefits consulting firm of Watson Wyatt found that 16 percent of these companies offered some sort of "phased retirement" plan. Fully 70 percent of the employers saw phased retirement as a possible solution to future labor shortages. A separate study, published in 1995, found that three out of four male workers over fifty years old wanted to reduce their work hours gradually instead of entering full retirement abruptly. (Diane W. Herz, "Work After Retirement: An Increasing Trend Among Men," *Monthly Labor Review*, April 1995.)

If you don't want to work for someone else, you may want to start your own small business or work as a freelancer or consultant. If you simply plan to become a consultant in your current field, the transition may be relatively smooth, but you may need to invest the time and money to go back to school for additional education and credentials.

SOME FINANCIAL FACTS OF POST-RETIREMENT WORK

As you consider whether and how to develop work opportunities that will continue into your golden years, keep in mind the following financial facts and make sure you understand how they may affect your income if you continue to work:

- You can start to receive Social Security at sixty-two, but the longer you wait, until age seventy, the higher your benefit will be.

- For anyone born after 1937, "normal retirement age"— at which you may receive your full Social Security benefit—will be sixty-six or older.

- If you earn "too much" money while receiving your Social Security benefit, your benefit could be reduced. Your additional post-retirement earnings can also increase your taxes.

#15

Delay Your Retirement.

People who have worked most or all of their lives may find it difficult to figure out when they are actually ready to retire. The decision may depend on a lot of factors—on attitudes about work and retirement, on family considerations, or on the need to be absolutely convinced that income that's been planned is sufficient.

"The real truth is that I am ready to retire now," admits Cathy. "But I have been too busy with my life and career to check things out and learn enough to know what's up financially."

Cathy recently passed the magic age of fifty-nine and a half, when she could start withdrawing money from her retirement accounts without paying a 10 percent penalty to the IRS. "But I have only recently reached a high salary and gotten out from under dependents, so I need to save now," this college professor says a bit ruefully.

Why does Cathy, a high-energy, prolific teacher and writer, want to retire early? "Illness unearths distress and awareness, and puts things in a different perspective," she says. "I always wanted to teach on and on, until I was eighty, but after I survived a life-threatening illness my notions changed. I wanted the time now, a retirement tempo that I didn't know whether I would have down the line. Even though I am an optimist about most things, I don't want to take a chance on waiting too long for the mental space of retirement." Another motive for retiring soon is to bail out of the "bureaucracy, administration, meetings, committees, arbitrary rules and regulations, hierarchy, and the fierce competition in academic life" and replace those activities with more focus on the creative side of her life—writing books and essays and "trying to make a difference" in her field.

As for her retirement lifestyle, Cathy's visions—she has a few of them—are pretty modest. One vision is living in her rustic cabin in the woods among friends, occasionally teaching a course at a nearby university, or taking some other type of part-time job to generate funds for traveling. Another vision is living in small towns in other countries, such as Spain or Mexico, in areas "that are not overrun with tourists and are accepting of outsiders." And then there's the fantasy of renting a trailer and simply parking it at her favorite spot overlooking the ocean.

On the brink of turning sixty, this college professor of twenty-seven years has retirement resources that many people would envy. She worked at major universities and built up a state-funded pension on one job and a retirement account of more than $350,000 at another. If she were to retire immediately, she would receive about $3,200 a month from the pension fund, a $40,000 additional lump sum from the state, and whatever income her $350,000 retirement account could generate. At a conservative 6 percent return on the retirement account, Cathy could increase her annual income by $21,000. By these estimates, she could retire on $59,400 a year now or $71,400 a year three years from now. Either figure would put her substantially above the average individual income in this country. Yet Cathy is committed to staying in a full-time job for a few more years. Why?

There is a purely economic consideration: If she keeps her present job for three more years, Cathy will increase her monthly pension income by about $600 to around $4,200. Another reason is more personal: Cathy says she's proud of having lived very frugally through her college years, but since then, she's gotten used to luxuries such as belonging to a gym and taking frequent airplane trips to visit her grandchild. Much as she would like to think she could live on a tight budget again, she still has doubts about her ability to do it. "It's just being risk averse after being an overspender and inattentive to money stuff. And not really getting the numbers, not getting the facts."

Cathy's story illustrates a fundamental truth about retirement planning and saving: Each person has to identify his or her own psychological as well as economic level of comfort and work toward achieving that goal. There is simply no cut-and-dried formula that will work for everyone.

#16

Evaluate Your Current Job's Retirement Benefits.

The computer age has brought massive changes to the American workplace—downsizing, demands for more highly skilled workers, increased mobility for workers. With these changes have also come changes in employee benefits. While the government requires employers to comply with certain rules in setting up and managing pension plans, any company has the right to change its retirement plan as long as the rules are followed. Here is how one woman who got caught in this type of change made sure that she would not have to work an extra fifteen years to catch up to the pension benefits she expected to receive from her job.

For twenty-three years, Joyce worked in computer-related jobs for a major corporation. For twenty-one years, her husband stayed home caring for their four children. This arrangement limited their retirement savings to what she could earn in her job, but Joyce didn't worry because the company had a good pension plan. In fact, she counted on being able to retire comfortably at age fifty-five.

Then one day when she was in her mid-forties, Joyce's employer announced that the company would replace its traditional plan with a new type of pension plan called a cash balance plan. With a traditional pension, the worker is guaranteed that after a certain number of years of service, he or she will receive a specific retirement income—say, $1,000 per month, or perhaps 60 percent of his or her final salary. With a cash balance plan, there is no such guarantee. Instead, the employer puts a sum of money—for example, 3 percent of salary—into a retirement savings account. The employer guarantees that the money will earn a certain amount—for example, 5 percent per year. But it is up to the worker to invest and manage the money. And, most important, there is no guarantee how much money will be in the account when the worker is ready to retire. If the money is not invested profitably, it could be much less than under the traditional pension.

Joyce was shocked when she learned about the new plan. It was hard to get detailed information from her employer about the impact that the cash balance plan would have on her retirement income. But Joyce is a skilled and determined professional, and she managed to get the figures she needed to compare the old and new plans. After crunching the numbers, she discovered the shocking truth: Under the new cash balance plan Joyce would have to work until age seventy to get the same benefits she would have received at age fifty-five from the traditional pension. "I started looking for information, trying to figure out if this was right, thinking something must be wrong with my paperwork," she recalls. "The more I looked into it, the angrier I got."

Although Joyce eventually found another job with better retirement benefits, her experience offers a cautionary note to others who have pension plans at their job: "Learn as much as you can as quickly as you can about your rights and what your individual company is doing. Most people don't take the time to do this," and if the employer makes a change—which is perfectly legal under federal law—"it may be too late to put alternative savings plans in place."

Joyce's experience reveals an important lesson: You should be aware not only of the retirement benefits you're currently entitled to, but also of whether—and how—your employer could change them with little or no notice. Joyce was fortunate to be offered another job with good retirement benefits, but others may not be as lucky, and should be prepared for all possibilities.

#17

Start a New Career.

Changing jobs is one thing, but making a midlife switch to a new career—that's definitely another level of commitment. These days, it's not that unusual. Most people will change careers at least once during their lifetime. We live in an era of lifelong learning. Many employers pay tens of thousands of dollars in tuition and expenses to enable their future managers to earn an MBA. Thousands of adults earn college degrees by taking courses over the Internet, or keep their skills current by attending continuing education programs in everything from counseling to law to medicine. Here's the story of one woman who decided at age fifty that, in order to have economic security when she retires, she needed to prepare herself for a totally new career.

"I've never been one to think about things like insurance or worry about my future," admits Marty, a fifty-four-year-old massage therapist.

She's worked all her life but never earned much and never really saved any money. This strong, resourceful woman has been an office worker, a hands-on woodworker, and an administrative assistant in a college admissions office. With one husband, she owned a Florida seafood restaurant, where she acted as the hostess and "out front" staff while her husband oversaw the kitchen. With another husband, she spent seven years in a historic town turning timeworn, two-hundred-year-old houses into charming residences. As if these work activities were not enough, over the same decades Marty raised three children and, for several years, lived in a primitive cabin—no electricity, with outdoor bathroom facilities—about sixteen hundred feet up on a mountainside.

And then she was fifty. For the first time, she started giving serious thought to her future. Marty and her husband both knew that they could not continue the demanding physical work of home renovation indefinitely. When Marty checked her Social Security record, she realized her credit for a long succession of part-time or seasonal, on-again, off-again jobs added up to only twelve years of earnings—a record that would provide a retirement benefit of about $300 a month unless she did something fairly dramatic to increase her income.

"I wanted to be self-supporting. My husband is eleven years older than I am, and I wanted something for myself in case something should happen to him. Years ago, when my kids were young, a chiropractor was revamping his office and he offered me his treatment table. He used it to do massage with friends, and to massage the kids. I started teaching myself and learning from friends." In college, Marty had taken all the prerequisites for graduate work in occupational therapy, so she'd been drawn to the idea of a career as a hands-on therapist for many years. All of these experiences added up to one answer: Become a certified massage therapist.

Four years later, Marty has completed a training course, passed her certification exam, completed advanced training, and built a thriving business of therapeutic massage in her town. It's been an intense four years, but she has no regrets. "Things look good. I am earning more money than ever before in my life," so that between now and age seventy, when she plans to retire, she'll increase her Social Security benefit substantially. For the first time, she's also going to start saving systematically, putting the money into a Simplified Employee Pension (SEP-IRA), a tax-deductible retirement savings account for people who are self-employed. When they gave up the home renovation business, her husband returned to a career he'd pursued many years before, as a social worker, at a job with a 401(k) retirement plan.

What about starting a new career at fifty? How hard is it? Marty points out that her fellow students in massage school ranged in age from their twenties to their sixties, proving that age does not have to be a barrier to a new career direction. "Learning the nuances of running a business—of taxes and forms—and figuring out how much you can charge for your services are a little challenging," she says. But what really counts, and what will enable you to make a successful career change, she counsels, is to make the right decision in the first place. "Pick something you really like to do, something that you give away for free, and get the training, and then just do it."

#18

Make Money Your New Business.

This may be the ultimate strategy for catching up on your retirement savings: When you choose a new career, consider opting for one that will immerse you in the world of money and investments.

"I went to work with the primary idea of building a retirement fund," declares Pamela, a certified financial planner who enrolled in college when she was forty-three years old and received a degree in economics when she was forty-eight. "My husband is a contractor who employs a number of workers," but she and her husband had no retirement plan. "If he started a SEP or Keogh (tax-favored retirement plans) for the business, he couldn't afford to do it for all the employees. So I saw it as my job to create a retirement plan for us," she explained.

Until she went to college, Pamela dedicated herself to raising their children. One financial expert says "you have two things to think about—education and retirement," Pamela recalled. "We had our children when we were very young and it worked out well. My husband was a savvy investor and we started college funds for them when they were very young. We never had to take money out of our own income to pay for their college."

Pamela's husband retired at sixty-two, collects his Social Security, plays a lot of tennis, and does the maintenance on their 110-acre property in New England. In the meantime, Pamela is sixty years old, working for a major brokerage firm and enjoying her work. She puts the maximum contribution into her 401(k) every year and is not in any hurry to retire. After all, she says, " I haven't worked very long. I love what I do. I will probably retire when I'm seventy."

#19

Become a Consultant in Your Field.

An increasingly common strategy to fill financial and other gaps in retirement life is extending your work years by becoming a consultant. By repackaging and marketing your skills, you can enhance your retirement income, yet retain the freedom to determine how much you want to work and under what circumstances—and you can even catch up by starting an IRA after you formally retire.

Eric is sixty-six and he's collecting Social Security. Last year he and his wife, Sheryl, who is ten years younger, started putting money into IRAs for the first time. They've been through some fits and starts in their financial lives, but one thing has remained consistent for Eric— he's always enhanced and built on his professional skills to generate an adequate income.

Eric began his career as a minister and then worked in the field of social services for the church. For thirty-eight years, the church contributed 8 percent of his salary to a pension plan and he put in 4 percent. When he was divorced after a twenty-five-year marriage, the only asset Eric had left was the money in the pension plan. Sheryl, his current wife, also works in social services. "The stress was phenomenal," he recalls. "One of us was traveling all the time." To deal with the stress of travel and separation, they decided that when Sheryl had to travel overseas for work, Eric would go along and they would tack some vacation time onto the work trip. This, of course, used up some of the income they might otherwise have saved for retirement. As work and financial pressure mounted, the vision of a new life in partial retirement began to emerge, Eric says: "Our dream was that we would start a consulting business, working with nonprofit organizations. The only thing we lacked was the money" to launch the business and pay for personal expenses.

One part of the vision was to reduce their expenses by living outside the city, but money was still enough of a problem that when they found the right house in the right town, Eric and Sheryl didn't have the full $20,000 they needed for the down payment. At the last minute, friends loaned them the missing $10,000 and they were able to get a mortgage and buy the house. Since they embarked on their small-town life and Eric started on Social Security, the consulting business has grown quickly, and at times they're working more than they'd really like to be. Their Social Security and pensions will enable this couple to live modestly in full retirement, but the successful consulting has also allowed them to start the IRAs so that they will have more resources to depend on when they want or need to reduce their workload.

#20

Start a New Business.

If you're tired of your previous job and want to seek new experiences and challenges as well as income, consider starting a new small business. To give yourself the best chance of success, pick a business that matches the retirement lifestyle you've chosen. This should protect you against the frustration of constantly having to choose between a business that overwhelms your schedule and your other retirement priorities, whether they are golf or travel or volunteer work.

Hannah, age sixty-one, is a divorced woman who works in a housing program for the Canadian government. The government pension she'll receive "will provide the basics, but I want a better lifestyle than just getting along." She's very clear about what that lifestyle should include: a base in North America, so she can stay in close touch with children and grandchildren; a climate that is not rainy and cool the way her home city in Canada is for six months of the year; and the financial security to travel to places, including "Portugal, Turkey, Bali, and London for the theater."

Currently, Hannah is intrigued by the idea of living in Ajijic, a community with many English-speaking North American expatriates, on Lake Chapala near Guadalajara, Mexico. "I went on a couple of real estate tours and talked with people there and determined that it would cost me about three-quarters of what it costs me here" to provide the basics for retirement, she says. But whether Hannah settles on Ajijic or another venue that's less expensive than her home city, she still will need more income than her pension to support the lifestyle she seeks. So at sixty-one years old, she's starting a new business—marketing through the Internet.

To get started, this civil servant has allied herself with two different companies. In both cases, the goal is to set up a network of distributors that is "strong and deep" and generates a large volume of sales, on which she would receive commissions. One company sells a diet product. The other, she says, sells a variety of products, "from skin moisturizer to golf clubs to Royal Doulton china." If her plans work out, the income from these new businesses will provide a healthy supplement to her government pension, and within a few years Hannah will be taking off for the exotic destinations that until now have only existed in her dreams. And the beauty of the Internet, of course, is that it will allow Hannah to carry her business with her, or at least monitor it from wherever she is on the globe.

#21

Prepare For or Find a "Bridge Job."

Even if you plan to work only a few more years before retiring, there may be good reasons—such as being bored or finding it impossible to get a raise—not to stay in your current job. This could be a signal to look for a bridge job—one that you will stay in for only a few years, maybe even at a part-time level, to keep the income flowing until you can afford to stop working altogether.

Janine is fifty years old and for about thirty years her work has required her to stand on her feet for nine hours or more every day. She's not quite ready to retire, but she's having back trouble, and she's definitely ready to get off her feet.

A hair stylist by training, as a young woman Janine worked for other employers in a beauty salons. Soon she saw, however, "that the owners weren't especially smart or talented. I figured if they had their own business, I could do that too."

With a colleague she had met in the course of her work, Janine decided to open her own salon in an affluent suburb of a major eastern city about fifteen years ago. The business was a great success. "We brought a few stylists with us from our other jobs, they were all very talented, and the business went bananas. At one point we were up to fifteen stylists working in the salon."

While working for other people, Janine never received any

pension benefits or saved money for retirement. "I concentrated on paying off my debts as soon as possible, not paying attention to income growth. I thought the secret was to be debt-free, but I found out that's not necessarily the way to go." That's because, having paid off her home mortgage, now she has virtually no tax deductions. Recently she's been thinking "a lot" about her future. One inspiration for making plans has been conversations with "a friend who is sixty-five and still working, and still very young at heart." As a result, Janine decided both to consult a financial adviser and to position herself for a bridge job that will allow her to sell the salon business but keep earning an income at a job that is less physically demanding.

For the last few years Janine has put $2,000 each year into an IRA, and "when I had extra money, I put it into mutual funds." The financial adviser has helped her shift that money to higher-yielding funds, with a goal of saving $200,000 before she retires. Currently she's trying to save as much as $25,000 per year for retirement.

Her plan is to sell her beauty salon business, probably in the next two years, because "the physical side of it is too hard." She knows she won't be able to afford to retire at that point, so Janine's other strategy is developing new skills that will qualify her to get a bridge job to produce income for at least a few years after she sells the business. She's started taking computer classes, already learning to do spreadsheets for her own business. When Janine sells the business, she'll look for a job "that is not too demanding, like office administration or some kind of computer work. It will be more like a phase-down than real retirement."

#22

Phase In Your Retirement.

As we live and remain healthy longer, the idea of an abrupt and total departure from work becomes less appealing to many people. A phased retirement can be the solution for people in two opposite situations: If you are at or close to normal retirement age, say sixty-five, and have not saved enough to be comfortable, you can cut your work back to part-time to supplement Social Security or pension income. But if you're younger, say in your fifties, and your retirement savings have boomed, phased retirement offers the chance to explore new personal and career avenues.

Jenny is one of the lucky ones in the second category. Early in her career a mentor told her that she should always max out contributions to her retirement accounts, that doing so would "only hurt once," when she made the decision. So month after month, year after year, money flowed automatically from Jenny's salary into her retirement funds. Jenny never really paid attention to how much had been accrued or what she might do with it. When she did take a careful look, she was fifty-six and the news was all good: she'd saved enough to collect a subsistence income and work only part-time.

In her early jobs, as an executive assistant and then in low-paid academic slots while attending graduate school, Jenny paid no attention to retirement. When she left an academic job after seven years at age thirty-six, she withdrew and spent the approximately $2,500 in her retirement account. "I thought it was use it or lose it," she explained. "Nobody told me I could roll it over into another retirement plan."

For the next twenty years Jenny worked as an executive for a nonprofit agency. That's when she got the invaluable advice about retirement savings from her mentor. Most of those years she thrived on her job, had a lot of freedom to pursue the work that interested her and benefited from access to inspiring colleagues. Then she got a new boss with a totally different view of the agency's function and an abrasive work style. Unable to accept the abrupt changes in the quality of her work life, Jenny negotiated a good severance package and resigned.

One of her first tasks after leaving was to conduct an in-depth analysis of her financial status. "I decided I had to know everything I had—all my sources of money. I decided to go to a financial planner for help, but I knew that I'd need detailed information on all of my assets and liabilities," so she started sifting through all of her financial records and organizing them. Very quickly Jenny discovered that she owed about $30,000 on several credit cards. Paying off the minimums every month—some at finance charges as high as 18 percent—she was making no progress on reducing the debt. Embarrassed at the prospect of seeking advice from a financial planner when she had so much credit card debt, Jenny immediately took some money out of a savings account to pay the debt on the cards down to $10,000.

In addition to debt, Jenny decided she needed to take control of "all the things I needed to be responsible for at this age: life insurance, health insurance, revising my will, estate planning, and providing for my teen-age daughter's college education." The biggest question revolved around the savings in her retirement account. She had $700,000, but she had no idea how far it would stretch. "I needed a projection for how to take care of myself and my family in the future."

When a friend and neighbor who works for a brokerage firm offered to help, Jenny took him up on the offer. "I thought I would just get some advice and transfer my funds" from the current accounts to his company. "I took him the balance sheet it had taken me at least two weeks to put together, went down and talked to him. It took about ten seconds for him to look at the balance sheet, congratulate me on the savings and ask me what I'd ideally like to do. I said I'd like to invest this money, get enough income to give me a base salary, and then do part-time consulting. He looked at me and said: 'When do you want to start?' "

Jenny thought she couldn't start at least until she was fifty-nine and a half and could take money out of her retirement accounts without incurring a 10 percent penalty. But the broker explained that she could avoid a penalty by using an alternative option that would allow her to start taking money from her IRA under a little-known, complex distribution formula for withdrawing money over five years or until she turned fifty-nine and a half. "He told me I could take 6.5 percent in income and assume an 11 to 13 percent annual growth rate in my investments—and that no one he had recommended this to in the past had ever lost money this way."

Since that day at the broker's about a year ago, Jenny receives enough income to pay the bills and has been luxuriating in thinking about what she calls the "third age" of her life. "The key thing is I have changed my definition of retirement. I don't think of literally 'retiring' per se any more. Instead I think of a gradual shift in the how much time I work and how much time I invest in other kinds of things—what I will do to earn money and what I really *like* to do." She hasn't arrived at a full-blown plan yet, but she's getting there. Already she's started to do some consulting and career coaching, and also to devote unpaid time to helping out some of the women's organizations whose work she admires and believes in.

TIPS

 If you're thinking about changing jobs, get the facts about the pension plan where you work now. If you have a traditional (defined benefit) pension plan, figure out how much your pension will increase if you stay longer in your current job. If you have a 401(k), 403(b), or 457 plan, you may withdraw the money in the fund if you change jobs, but if you are younger than fifty-nine and a half, you must roll the money over into an Individual Retirement Account or other tax-favored pension plan within sixty days or you'll be charged a 10 percent penalty plus income tax by the IRS. To learn how your pension plan works and what you are entitled to, ask your employer for these two documents, which the company is required by law to provide:

1. Summary Plan Description: This document describes the plan rules and procedures.

2. Individual Benefit Statement: You are entitled to request and receive a copy of your own benefit statement once a year.

If your employer is not willing to give you these documents, contact the Division of Assistance and Inquiries, U.S. Department of Labor, by calling 202-219-8776.

 Get the facts about how continuing to work can affect your Social Security benefit. Here's how to get the information:

- Call the Social Security toll-free number, 800-772-1213. Read publications on the Internet at http://www.ssa.gov. Visit your local Social Security office to speak with a staff person about your own personal situation. You can locate the office on the Internet site or by looking in your local phone book under "U.S. Government."

☑ **If you're thinking about working after you retire, get reliable tax advice.** As long as you have earnings, you'll need to pay the FICA (Social Security and Medicare) tax on that income up to $84,900 (in 2002; the amount increases each year). If you're employed, your contribution is 7.65 percent; if you're self-employed, it's 15.3 percent.

☑ **Learn how the earnings limit may affect your Social Security benefit.**

- If you're on Social Security, are younger than age 65, and still working, in 2002 you can earn $30,000 without having your benefit reduced. But if you earn more and you're under age sixty-five, you will lose $1 for every $2 you earn above the limit. However, as a result of a recent change in the law, the earnings limit for retirees who are age sixty-five to sixty-nine has been repealed, so people in this category who continue to work will no longer have to worry about losing part of their Social Security benefit. To make sure that you will not suffer financially from working while on Social Security, consult your accountant or tax lawyer.

☑ **Don't become a victim of age discrimination.** In a company with at least twenty employees, it's against the law for an employer to discriminate against you in areas including hiring, firing, pension, and other benefits, and employers who offer an early retirement package must follow federal guidelines to ensure that they do not discriminate. If you suspect that your age is the reason you're being denied a job, a promotion, or higher benefits, here's what you can do about it:

- Contact the Equal Employment Opportunity Commission (EEOC), which enforces the federal age discrimination law, by calling 202-663-4900, or read about age discrimination law on the EEOC website, http://www.eeoc.gov.

- For information on opportunities for older workers, as well as on their legal rights, contact the Federal Administration on Aging by writing to the National Aging Information Center (NAIC), 330 Independence Ave. S.W., Washington, D.C. 20201; by calling the NAIC at 202-619-0724; sending an e-mail to naic@aoa.gov; or by going to http://www.aoa.dhhs.gov/seniorjobs/default.htm. Also, visit the AARP website at http://www.aarp.org/indexes/money.html#working.

CHAPTER FOUR

DOWNSIZE
YOUR LIFE NOW
(TO INCREASE YOUR SAVINGS)

Let's say that every morning on the way to work you pick up a caffe latte, which costs you $3. That means you've spent $15 for each five-day week, or $750 per fifty-week work year. If you simply didn't spend that money for thirty years, you'd have $22,500 to spend for retirement. And that's without any interest.

Late in the 1990s some organizations that were promoting retirement savings came up with this example to show that every budget has some slack in it that could be put away for retirement—if you are willing to make the decision to save.

One of the most fundamental reasons that people need to catch up on retirement savings is that they are spending all of their money as fast as—or even faster than—it comes in. In some cases, they live beyond their means, going deeper and deeper into debt. The 1990s produced an economic boom that for many families could justify increased spending on non-necessities. But often people simply don't pay attention to how much they're spending until it's too late; or they continue on a spending spree even though on some subconscious level they may know that the boom will not last forever.

The evidence of this attitude is widespread. Credit card debt has a way of creeping up on us. Now that plastic can be used for everything from college tuition to doctor bills or even to pay taxes, there's more potential for creeping than ever. According to the Consumer Federation of America, in 1997, 55 to 60 percent of all American households had unpaid credit card debt. The average size of the debt was $7,000, and the average annual cost of interest and fees on the debt was $1,000. Those who ultimately give up on paying all their debts declare bankruptcy, which has become more and more common. The American Bankruptcy Institute reports that in 2000 nearly 1.3 million people filed for personal bankruptcy.

For most people who need to catch up on retirement savings, the key to finding money to save is cutting back on current expenses. But how to do that is not always obvious. We all become accustomed to certain routines—like drinking a latte every morning—to structure the daily life we want.

So where do you begin to downsize your life? To find the slack in your budget, you'll need to take four steps:

1. Make an accurate, complete list of your expenses.
2. Make a list of your income, your assets, and your liabilities.
3. Compare your annual expenses with your income.
4. Examine your expenses in depth and create a budget you can live with.

STEP 1:
MAKE AN ACCURATE, COMPLETE LIST OF YOUR EXPENSES.

Start by keeping a written record of all the money you spend for a month, perhaps in a notebook you carry in your purse or pocket.

The amount you spend on rent or mortgage, health insurance, or utility bills probably doesn't vary much. But do you really know where all the cash you take out of the ATM is going? To get a complete picture, you should try to record every single expense—lunches, cleaning, parking fees or gas, pet food, haircuts, fitness club dues, and minimum payments required on credit card debt or any other types of loans.

Also make a list of annual or other one-time expenses. This category should include items such as all of your insurance (assuming you don't pay it every month), membership or dues in organizations, medical bills, furniture or home repairs, and vacations. And don't forget to add taxes—federal and state income tax and property, business, or other local levies. For some sources that can help you create your own complete list of expenses, see the "Tips" section of this chapter. Once you've made your lists, here's what you do:

1. Total your monthly expenses and multiply by 12.
2. Total your annual or one-time expenses.
3. Add the two totals to arrive at your total annual expenses.

STEP 2:
MAKE A LIST OF YOUR INCOME, ASSETS, AND LIABILITIES.

In addition to salary or self-employment income, include interest and dividends from bank accounts, money market earnings, other investment income, and if you are a landlord, rental income. If you have a trust fund, put that income down, too.

STEP 3:
COMPARE YOUR ANNUAL EXPENSES WITH YOUR INCOME.

Look at the big picture. Are you consistently spending more than you earn? Have you included a regular contribution to retirement savings in your expenses? Are you paying off debt or just juggling from month to month? Are you paying off debt at the most favorable rates available to you?

STEP 4:
EXAMINE YOUR EXPENSES, ONE BY ONE,
AND CREATE A BUDGET YOU CAN LIVE WITH.

Budgeting of course requires you to set priorities, to make choices, to put an end to impulse spending, and to simply downsize some of your spending on a regular basis.

Perhaps you and your spouse each commute to work in separate vehicles that cost you for gas, insurance, maintenance, and parking. Yet you live near the subway that goes within two blocks of your office. Do you really need both cars? Compare the costs of subway commuting and driving your own car. Even if you take a taxi home a couple of evenings a month, the savings from living with one car instead of two could be substantial.

How many nights a week do you eat in a restaurant or buy take-out food? The convenience of not cooking all your meals can exact a heavy price. Is there some way you can prepare food on the weekend that can be served for dinner some evenings during the week?

These are only a couple of examples. In this chapter you'll learn about many more creative steps that other people like yourself have taken to reduce their spending.

But there's a second aspect of budgeting that is also very important and may even save you more money: managing your finances better. Here are some examples:

- Reduce your taxes. For example, if you owe estimated taxes, pre-pay items such as your January mortgage and your state taxes in December so that they'll count as deductions for that year. If you don't have a tax adviser, then get one who will help you identify other tax savings. With your broker or other financial adviser, review your portfolio to see if you should shift some of your investments into more tax-advantaged vehicles.

- Reduce your mortgage payments. If you bought your house, say, ten years ago, you may be paying much higher rates than you need to pay now. Check into options for refinancing. Just make sure that when you do the calculations, you wrap the closing costs you'll have to pay into the bottom line estimate.

- Reorganize your debt to pay lower finance charges. It's not uncommon to have debt on several credit cards, each with a different interest rate. Maybe you transferred a credit card balance from one account to another when you got a good deal two years ago—but now the rate has gone up from 4 percent to 18 percent. Make a list of the cards, how much you owe on each one, and the rate you're paying. Then try to transfer whatever debt you can't pay now to cards with lower rates. Sometimes you can consolidate all of the debt onto one card with a lower rate. If you have a lot of home equity, you may be able to shift the debt to a home equity loan instead.

If you are serious about catching up on saving for retirement, downsizing will almost certainly be one of the strategies you employ. Maybe all you'll need to do is refinance the house, and put the savings into your retirement account every month. Or if you're very close to retirement and your savings are very low, maybe you'll need to make a lot of changes in your spending habits—possibly even move to a less expensive apartment, or spend your vacations at home for the next few years instead of at a ski lodge or on a game safari.

It's like choosing a diet. Some people lose weight by drinking a vitamin cocktail for two out of three meals a day. Others take off pounds by reducing their caloric intake or their consumption of fats or carbohydrates. As with a food diet, what counts when you downsize your living expenses is that you stick to your plan.

All of the people featured in this chapter have found one or more ways to cut their expenses so that they can devote more savings to their retirement funds. Some of their strategies require relatively sophisticated financial research and even professional guidance. Others are strategies you can easily adopt yourself, just by increasing your awareness of what you spend and resolving that you will not allow that spending to get out of control.

#23

Shift Debt from High-Interest Credit Cards to a Mortgage or Home Equity Loan.

When you face a constant barrage of credit card finance charges and the debt never seems to go down, it can be pretty hard to squeeze out a monthly contribution to your retirement account. That's why sometimes the first step toward building up your retirement savings is to pay off the credit cards—or at least to come up with a plan that allows you to reduce the debt and save for retirement at the same time.

At forty-nine years old, David was a self-employed lawyer with about $100,000 in credit card debt. About $10,000 of the debt was on a card that charged 14.9 percent, and the rest was on cards with finance charges of 17 percent. A divorced father who has custody of his son, David had piled up the debt as a result of a costly divorce settlement, buying out a business partner, and paying bills his ex-wife had incurred as a result of her addiction to making purchases from the television shopping channels.

Now he was stuck trying to pay off the debt, create a college fund for his ten-year-old, and add to the $120,000 he had put into Keogh and IRA retirement accounts in the past. These goals were not easy to achieve, because his income was unpredictable and fluctuated widely—from $17,000 in one recent year to $150,000 in 1999.

A financial adviser ran the numbers reflecting David's situation through accounting software. He recommended two steps David could take to reduce his monthly expenses: wrap some of the credit card debt into a loan that would refinance his house; and consolidate the remaining debt onto cards with lower interest rates.

David owed about $125,000 on his mortgage and was paying a rate of 7⅞ percent per year. When he asked his bank for refinancing, the answer was: "When you originally got this mortgage, you had two incomes. But now you're single, and you're an entrepreneur with a sole proprietorship." They considered it too risky to give him the new mortgage. The second mortgage company David approached had a very different attitude: "We know that if you default on this loan, you'll lose your license" to practice law, they said, so they did not see him as a serious risk. Within a month, David had increased his mortgage to $195,000. The house was worth considerably over $200,000, so the lender allowed him to wrap $70,000 of credit card debt into the new mortgage, which he pays at a rate of 7¾ percent.

The next step was to reduce the finance charges on the other $30,000 of credit card debt. When David called up the credit card company, he asked for a rate of 9.9 percent, which he knew they were offering. To his surprise, they even offered to guarantee him that rate "in perpetuity."

Just two or three years before, David seemed to be mired in financial disaster. Although he had a nice start on building up retirement savings, his debts were so high that he couldn't imagine taking money out of cash flow to save for the future. But by refinancing the house, wrapping in some of the credit card debt, and getting a lower rate on the remaining debt, "I've reduced my out-of-pocket expenses by about $1,500 a month," a tidy $18,000 a year. With the divorce and changes in his business completed, David's earnings went way up in 1999, enabling him to pay off $15,000 or half of his remaining credit card bills and to fully fund his son's college education by contributing to a program offered to residents of the state where he lives.

And David is reaping yet another bonus from all of this financial housecleaning: a much lower tax rate in a year when his income was high. That's because the credit card interest that was shifted to the mortgage is now deductible, as are the large costs he spent on dissolving his business partnership. And now, after several years of uncertainty and crisis, David is also in a position to use his higher earnings to catch up on contributions to his retirement account—instead of on finance charges to credit card companies.

#24

Make Frugality a Way of Life.

Life really consists of a seemingly endless parade of choices we make. Sometimes we're conscious of those choices, and sometimes we're not. With the boost provided by technology, many Americans are choosing to work for themselves—often in a home office—instead of for an employer who has the power to determine their personal schedule and priorities as well as their salary. Especially during the first years on their own, many self-employed people pay for their freedom with major financial sacrifices. In this case, a committed freelancer has made the conscious decision that, in order to start saving for retirement, she must cut back on every possible expense, from furniture to clothing to transportation.

"Am I concerned about catching up with my retirement savings? Try 'freaked out.' 'Panicked.' Or 'very, very nervous.'" That's what Patricia said when she was interviewed about her financial prospects for the future.

"With my stock, mutual funds portfolio, and SEP/IRA, I am worth only about $35,000. And you bet that concerns me. I'm forty-three. Even if there weren't so many twenty-something millionaires around me, I'd be painfully aware that I am not doing well enough to ensure even a sparse retirement," she continues.

Patricia's had a terrific career in high tech, and she's also turned down some terrific career opportunities—jobs that would have paid her considerably more than $100,000 a year. So what's the problem?

Like many people, she had a few jobs in the years after college that did not offer any pension credit. The salaries were low, and even when she worked for a major corporation for a year, she didn't stay long enough to earn retirement benefits. "I did not get into the habit of saving when I should have, with those first jobs. I owed about $10,000 in student loans, and no one told me you should be paying off your loans and saving money concurrently."

During the five years that Patricia worked for a major corporation the company started a 401(k), matching every dollar she put into the account with fifty cents. Although Patricia was better now about saving money, her focus was more on creating a stash for big purchases, such as furniture, or for treats such as travel, rather than for retirement. For many years it didn't occur to her that she might have to be responsible for her own financial future. "Until I was in my late thirties, I didn't clue in to the possibility that I might not get married. I didn't assume that a husband would take care of me, but I come from a family where marriage at some point was 'programmed' into me. Besides, I thought spending my money, not saving it, was an independent, empowered, single-woman act."

Turning down offers for lucrative jobs with generous benefits, in 1992 she decided to leave the corporate world and try to make it as a freelance consultant. Two months later she was diagnosed with carpal tunnel syndrome—the wrist condition that is an occupational hazard for people who work a lot on computers. Disabled for eight months, Patricia used up $10,000 in savings plus $2,000 her mother contributed to her expenses. Even after the carpal tunnel problem improved, she learned that this was only one symptom of chronic fatigue syndrome, a disease that she controls now with medication but which restricts her ability to work on a regular schedule or on the eighty-hour-a-week corporate schedule she had led for several years before quitting.

Ever since becoming self-employed, Patricia has been treading water financially. With the help of a financial consultant, she has set up a system to make sure she sets aside money to pay her taxes and to contribute $3,000 or $4,000 a year to her SEP. And she's consciously committed herself to frugality in almost every aspect of her daily life. What exactly are her strategies? Here are some of them:

- "Cut down on spending." She limits long-distance calls to business contacts, survives without a cell phone, and restricts travel expenses by using frequent flyer miles and visiting friends. Entertainment costs are almost nil—"$7.75 for a movie—are they kidding?" While on a trip to the beach in Delaware during the summer, she did her Christmas shopping at factory outlet stores to benefit from the discounts and avoid sales taxes. (There are none in that state.)

- "Use things up." Patricia drives a 1990 Geo Prizm with 70,000 miles on it. Her living room couch has been "shredded" by the cat, but she's not about to replace it. "I recycle everything, from wrapping paper to gifts." She stretches her clothing budget as far as possible—buying only what she needs to look respectable for business appointments, and donating the old stuff to charity to get a tax break.

- "Consolidate high-interest loans and pay them off." Combining two credit card debts that had interest rates of up to 18.5 percent at times, on a card with a 10.9 percent rate that she was offered in the mail, Patricia has reduced the debt from about $6,000 to $2,500.

While these strategies are helping Patricia at least put some money into her retirement accounts, she still has plenty

of "financial anxiety." Some of this results from being surrounded by a boom economy. "Everyone I know is better off
than I am, whether from two incomes, a wealthy spouse, investments, inheritances—even divorce settlements. People are
suspicious when I say I can't go out to dinner because finances
are tight." Many of these people don't understand that she
considers her freelancing a career, not a hobby, that she works
at least as hard as they do in conventional jobs, and that she'll
never finish the book she is currently writing unless she can
maintain control of her own schedule.

So that's where her next catch-up strategy comes in: Patricia has decided that she's going to learn how to save money
even more effectively, and also to invest. "To have enough
money to make money," she observes. "That's a concept." And
in this book, that's also another chapter.

#25

Give Up Some Luxuries.

One person's luxury may be another's necessary expense. Yet when financial crisis looms, somehow we begin to redefine what is really necessary. Among the "necessities" that the family in this story paid for was helping out their relatives. When they both lost their jobs, they realized they had to cut back not only on luxuries, but also on what they thought had been "necessities."

Sylvia had a good job with an advertising agency, but when the agency lost a big account in 1987, she lost her job. Of the $117,000 lump sum she got from her profit-sharing plan when she left the job, Sylvia rolled over $35,000 into an IRA and used the rest to pay off debts resulting—among other things—from recently having bought a new house and from helping out other family members with their financial problems. Then her husband, Don, was also laid off from his work in the telecommunications industry.

The next few years were very difficult. She and her husband took a series of part-time and temporary jobs. At one point he sold cars and she worked as a clerk in a department store. They were also supporting a teenage daughter, and Don ended up in the hospital, incurring thousands of dollars in bills, when he had no health insurance. In this period they were taking money out of the IRA whenever they had bills to pay. They closed off part of their four–bedroom, 3,200–square foot-home to reduce the bills for heating. They put the house on the market, but the market was slow. "We had taken out a home equity loan to tide us over," Sylvia recalls, "and when the house was finally sold twenty months later, we used the profit to pay off the loan and other bills and to buy a new, smaller house."

Finally, Don got a job, with less salary and fewer benefits than he was used to, but at least there were benefits, including a pension. He stayed in the job, underemployed, until retiring in 1998 at age sixty-seven. When he retired, he was able to collect about $1,230 a month in Social Security and about $270 from a pension.

In the meantime, Sylvia, who is ten years younger than Don, had found a public relations job that used her skills and experience. She immediately started putting 3 percent of her salary into the company's retirement fund. After gaining some financial stability, she upped the contribution to 5 percent of her salary.

Because they are still paying off their debts and want to step up their savings, Sylvia and Don made a conscious decision to give up some luxuries. "We were big diners-out. We used to spend $100 at dinner and we don't do that anymore. Now we're not averse to stopping at McDonald's for dinner instead," Sylvia says. "I used to wear designer clothes. Now I shop at the thrift shop. We used to have about nine credit cards. Now I've cut back to three. I don't want any increased credit card limits."

As for entertainment, Sylvia says "we're movie buffs, but we go to early movies because they are cheaper and we can get senior citizen rates. We now ask for senior citizen rates for everything—airplanes, hotel rooms, even dinners." And after many years of doling out money to children and nieces and nephews for everything from plane tickets to ballet lessons, Sylvia says, "we've decided that we can't be the family bank anymore."

Despite being "retired," Don has found a part-time job supervising home renovation workers. He's putting all the money he earns into an IRA for the future.

All in all, Sylvia and Don are feeling much better about their retirement lifestyle options now than at any time in the last decade. They haven't come up with a detailed budget based on their income when Sylvia leaves her job, but they plan to do that soon. "There are a lot of things we want to do," says Sylvia, such as travel and possibly move to a warmer climate. A few years ago, achieving these goals was unthinkable. Now that this couple has moved from financial crisis to a situation where they are in control of their money, "we're looking back at ourselves" and at the experience of the last decade or more, "keeping in mind that we are both professionals who worked all of our lives . . . and wondering what the hell happened to us," comments Sylvia. While they may never be able to sort out all the factors that led to their financial crises, she realizes that what's important is they've made some lifestyle changes that for the first time offer them the prospect of a financially secure retirement when they both decide to stop working altogether.

#26

An Extreme Case: Declare Bankruptcy.

This strategy is not a recommendation from the author. But there are some people in our society who—whether because of personal calamity or just plain indifference and self-deception about their financial life—conclude that the only way to recoup financially is to declare bankruptcy. The repercussions of bankruptcy can be severe—difficulty in obtaining credit, higher finance charges on credit cards that you can qualify for, and higher down payment requirements should you want to buy a home. Also, legislation pending in Congress could make it more difficult to declare bankruptcy on consumer debt.

THIS STORY COMES FROM A FINANCIAL PLANNER.

Drew was one of those apparently successful doctors you always hear about. He had a nice lifestyle: a million-dollar house, a leased Lexus, vacations in France, and a brokerage account with which he played the stock market.

He also had a lot of expenses, including a private medical practice that did not make a profit and $50,000 a year in private school tuition fees for his two children.

At age forty-four, Drew had decided that his retirement goal was to have $100,000 in annual income and stop working at fifty-five. Already his expectations were unrealistic, because at that time, he'd saved only $20,000 and was in debt. When he was fifty, he went to see a financial planner because although he was approaching retirement age quickly, his finances clearly were not going to support his goal. The planner reviewed all of Drew's assets and liabilities and the result was stark: $800,000 in debt. Technically, Drew had a net worth of $300,000, but because it was based on an unprofitable medical practice, his adviser explains, even that amount did not really "count" as an asset.

One strategy for salvaging Drew's financial future was to shape up his business. "Drew was losing a lot of money by accepting Medicare patients, so I recommended that he stop taking them," his financial adviser said. "He also had to limit vacation time to two weeks for all of his employees, replace some employees who were not productive, and delineate who would handle the money in the office to get expenses under better control."

But these changes in the business were simply not going to be enough. What Drew really had to do was downsize the family's opulent lifestyle. Drew agreed to get rid of the $1,000-a-month Lexus lease and get a more economical car, refrain from stock market ventures, and sacrifice the European vacation trips. With his adviser, they set priorities for paying off the debt, which included about $130,000 in credit cards. The monthly tab for paying the mortgage and the credit card debt came to $11,000.

A key to making this financial plan work was selling the big, expensive house. Drew and his wife put it on the market and kept lowering the asking price, but there simply were no buyers at a price anywhere near what they needed.

Two years after Drew had gone to the financial adviser, the only alternative he could find for climbing out of debt was to declare bankruptcy. The family lost the house, wrote off the credit card debts, and moved into a smaller home. Drew opened up a pension plan for his medical practice and is stashing away as much of his income as possible—up to $75,000 per year—to work toward his goal of accumulating $1.7 million for retirement.

Drew got into financial trouble because he did not pay attention to the money side of his life. "When he saw the complete picture," his financial adviser recalls, "he said: 'I'm glad you showed me. I wanted to know.' He was a physician and he knew something was wrong, but he just couldn't see it." For the most part, Drew has followed the expert advice he received. But there's one exception: He still wants to play the stock market, which in the past has not been a good financial move for him. Whether he is ultimately successful in catching up on his retirement savings may depend more on his activities in the market than on his declaration of bankruptcy.

#27

Save 10 Percent of Every Paycheck for Retirement.

One way to cut expenses is to make a budget that allocates cuts to various categories of disposable income, such as clothing, eating out, or vacations. Another way is to set a dollar limit on your spending and discipline yourself to stick to it.

Stephanie was only thirty-five when she started saving to catch up for retirement. This might seem like a tender age at which to declare yourself behind, but her case was special: Stephanie was catching up for her mother as well as for herself. "I thought my mother was going to break up with my father. They have separated since. I realized that I had to start saving, not just for myself, but for her, in case she needed money. That was the really pivotal event."

Now Stephanie is thirty-nine. Her mother emerged from her divorce with the family home and a portion of her ex-husband's pension. So far Stephanie has not had to help her financially, although she might have to do so if her mother developed a serious health problem. In the meantime, Stephanie upped her own retirement savings from $25,000 in 1996 to about $112,000 four years later.

Like Frank Sinatra, she's done it "her way"—by forcing herself to put 10 percent of every paycheck into a retirement fund. This strategy came to Stephanie after she read a money management book by Andrew Tobias. "There were two ways listed on how to budget," she recalls. "One had you draw up a big list of your expenses and chart up the income and outgo. That idea seemed like too much work. The next idea took one paragraph only: It was something like, 'Decide to save 10 percent of your income. Take it out immediately from your paycheck. . . . Force yourself to live within your means, with the rest of the paycheck.'"

Stephanie has not always been a dedicated saver. "In my earlier days, I used to spend like a crazy person. I had no idea what money was left, and where it was going. Thus I was always using my credit cards and feeling a bit stressed out." When she first vowed to save 10 percent of her salary, Stephanie was living in New York and working as a manager in a multinational firm. "It was quite tough. I stopped taking taxis, I cut way back on my purchases of books from Barnes and Noble, I cooked more at home, I almost literally stopped buying clothes," she recalls.

Now she and her husband live and work in Bangkok, but she has stuck to the money diet. Living in Asia has inspired her to observe the financial regimen in at least two ways. One was negative, when she saw the impact of the drop in Asian financial markets at close hand. "I could see right in front of me how awful it was for people living in the same city who got wiped out financially." The other stimulus from living in Asia was positive: "Asians save a ton of money, to their credit; there is no bank insurance like we have in the States with the FDIC."

After depositing 10 percent of her paycheck in mutual funds, Stephanie starts each pay period with a specified amount of cash in her pocket to spend. "If I eat at very expensive Italian restaurants, say ten times, early in the month, then late in the month it's slim pickings. Or if I have a big vacation trip somewhere in Asia, then again I just force myself to live on what's left." Credit card spending is verboten, except for business expenses that will be reimbursed. "If you do not operate on a cash basis all of the time, it is hard to feel that the money is gone. This is how people get into credit card trouble. They psychologically believe that the credit card 'advance' of money to them is actually a gift, not a loan."

Stephanie's general goal is to save a million dollars befoi she retires, but "it's more the percentage of each paycheck tha I am pretty firm about," she says. When and where they'll re tire and what they'll be doing, Stephanie and her husband ar not sure yet. And it's no wonder, because there are plenty o other things to think about first: In addition to the 10 perceni of paycheck that she puts into her retirement fund, he contributes to his own retirement savings, and they are also saving $500 a month to buy a house when they return to the U.S. and $400 per month to the college education fund of the baby that's "not even a glimmer" in their eyes yet.

But then, what else would you expect from a woman who declares: "My idea of a great day is Saturday morning: I pull out all my bank books and checks to see which checks have cleared and which haven't and what's the balance." And then, for a little more fun, she turns to the funds that hold her retirement accounts and checks out their progress, too.

TIPS

☑ **Calculate all of your expenses and income.** For formats you can use, check out http://www.kiplinger.com/managing/cash/budget on the Internet. If you don't have access to the Internet, a good general finance book that includes forms you can use is:

- *Let's Talk Money,* by Dee Lee and David Caruso (Chandler House Press, 1999).

☑ **Optimize your credit cards.** To search for the best current credit card rates, check out:

- http://www.bankrate.com

- Kiplinger's website (URL above). There's a monthly update on the best cards in *Kiplinger's Personal Finance* magazine, available on newsstands.

☑ **Institute a plan to reduce spending.** Check the following websites for innovative approaches to reducing spending, as well as how to budget and manage cash flow. At some of these sites you can sign up to receive an e-mail newsletter with a constant stream of cost-cutting suggestions:

- http://www.stretcher.com

- http://www.slnet.com

☑ **First educate yourself about bankruptcy if you are considering this option.** For basic consumer-oriented information on bankruptcy, go to:

- http://www.abiworld.org, the site of the American Bankruptcy Institute. To contact the Institute offline, call them at 703-739-0800, or write them at 44 Canal Center Plaza, Suite 404, Alexandria, VA 22314.

CHAPTER FIVE

MAKE THE MOST OF YOUR HOME EQUITY

It's common to be sentimentally attached to your own home. But when you're planning for retirement—and you need to catch up on your finances—it's time to give up the idea that your house is simply a place to live.

For most Americans, the home they live in is their most valuable financial asset. In 1999, two-thirds of all Americans owned their homes. For people aged forty-five to fifty-four, the rate is 76 percent. For those aged fifty-five to sixty-four, it's 81 percent; and for those sixty-five or older, the rate is 80 percent.

But unless you've had the misfortune to buy a house in a neighborhood that has deteriorated significantly, the bricks and mortar structure has a value beyond the cost of the materials. Even if you don't own your house outright, you can still make use of the investment—known as equity—that you have paid toward owning it outright.

If you need to catch up on your retirement savings, home equity is an asset that you can exploit—an asset that can be manipulated to your financial advantage in many different ways. However, not many Americans are inclined to do this. The 1998 Fannie Mae National Housing Survey found that "Americans tend to be conservative when it comes to the equity in their homes." For example, 45 percent of participants—all baby boomers—said they'd prefer to have a higher mortgage payment with a shorter term, instead of a lower mortgage payment over a longer period. Only 12 percent of those interviewed said they would "be likely to tap the equity in their homes" for the purpose of adding to retirement savings, compared to 42 percent who said they might do so for a home renovation or to help pay a child's college expenses.

Lois Finkelstein, a Washington, D.C., attorney who specializes in family law, has observed a similar phenomenon among many women she's represented in divorce cases. "Women of all ages seem to be attached to their homes and willing to give up a major share of potential retirement assets" for the sake of keeping the home in a divorce settlement, she says. But it often makes more financial sense, Finkelstein suggests, to negotiate a settlement that disposes of the home where the marriage broke up and focuses more on collecting assets from the couple's 401(k) or IRAs.

Tim Corliss, a California realtor who specializes in working with clients on how to organize their financial life for retirement, also thinks that the Americans are often short-sighted when they insist on living in their same home after retirement. The founding director of the Senior Advantage Real Estate Council, Corliss is a California realtor who specializes in working with clients who are grappling with how to organize their financial life in retirement. He even started an organization and developed a course that offers professional credentials—SRES, or Senior Real Estate Specialist—to agents who want to specialize in counseling pre-retirees and retirees on their real estate needs. Corliss says that one of the most common mistakes people make in financial planning for retirement is failing to recognize the true economic value of their home. By this, he means how much you could earn on the equity if you took it out of your house and invested it elsewhere.

For example, let's say that you're fifty years old and you own a house that's worth $300,000 on the market. A reasonable current return on another type of investment of that size would be 8 percent—$24,000 a year or $2,000 a month. But you are still paying $900 a month on your original mortgage. Corliss would argue that the cost of continuing to live in your house is not just $900 a month, but $2,900—your mortgage payment plus the $2,000 a month you lose by not investing the home equity elsewhere. If you sold the house, there are several things you could do with the $300,000. These include spending part of proceeds to buy a less expensive home, perhaps one worth $200,000, and investing the rest for retirement; or put 50 percent down on a small multifamily unit such as a duplex or a triplex where you could live as an owner, collect rent from one or more tenants, and put the profit into a retirement fund. Corliss suggests that if you don't want to leave your current neighborhood, chances are that if you look carefully, you might even find this type of small investment property in the same area.

As you're planning your retirement catch-up, another option you may want to investigate is the possibility of securing a reverse mortgage—yet another strategy for exploiting your home equity. A reverse mortgage differs from a conventional mortgage in the following ways:

- You may continue to live in the home until you die without making any mortgage payments;
- You receive money in one of three forms—monthly payments, a lump sum, or access to a line of credit, based on the amount of equity you had in your home; and
- When you die, the home is sold to pay off the mortgage.

These advantages, of course, have costs associated with them—the usual closing costs such as fees for a title search and inspection—as well as interest. These costs—as well as the amount of money you can receive—can vary significantly depending on your choice of lender. If you do not plan to remain in your home for the rest of your life, paying off the loan yourself could be an expensive proposition.

Because reverse mortgages are so complex, it is essential to get expert help before deciding whether to apply, as well as before choosing the one that is best for you. (See the "Tips" section at the end of this chapter for sources of information.)

Finally, in considering whether to sell your home to catch up on your retirement savings, don't forget that Uncle Sam has an offer for you that will be very hard to refuse: As long as the home has been your principal residence for two out of the last five years, you may extract up to $250,000 in tax-free profit for it if you are single, and $500,000 in tax-free profit for a married couple. That's a benefit that you definitely will not receive if you start selling off your stocks and bonds to finance your retirement.

#28

Speed Up Paying Off Your Mortgage So That You'll Own Your Home Outright When You Retire.

Often the first thing that comes to mind in retirement planning is paying off your home mortgage. The advantages to this strategy may be the psychological comfort of having a debt- and rent-free place to live, and the possibility of keeping the maximum profit if you should decide to sell the house or apartment.

However, paying off the mortgage is not necessarily the best financial move for everybody. One reason is that you may stand to lose substantial tax benefits from the home mortgage deduction. Another is that some mortgages penalize you for early payoff, and/or impose special fees for doing this. On the other hand, if your agreement allows for it, sometimes making as little as one additional payment a year can take years off a thirty-year mortgage. If you're tempted to make a mortgage payoff a priority, make sure that you know what the impact will be on your entire financial situation. Then make a decision based on both the financial impact and your personal comfort level.

About fifteen years ago, Steve's retirement finances looked pretty good, partly because he had inherited a brokerage account from his parents. Then he became embroiled in divorce proceedings that lasted for nearly ten years. By 1996 when the divorce became final, says this fifty-eight-year-old scientist, he'd "wiped out over $300,000 in cash," buying out his ex-wife's interest in their home and his business. "That money would have made a reasonable start on retirement," he points out.

Now he's trying to figure out if he will *ever* be able to afford to retire. "My only serious hope for retirement now," he says, "is to maintain my health and continue working."

Early in his career Steve was employed as a research scientist for a few years each for two different companies. When he left the second company after five years, he recalls, "there was a small retirement payout, but no accumulation" that was significant. He doesn't recall how he spent the money.

Since 1978 Steve has owned a 50 percent share of a small company that sells scientific equipment. After ten years, the business started to suffer from changes in the marketplace and distribution systems. "Our best year was 1988 and we've been going slowly downhill ever since. It's been a constant struggle to stay afloat. Setting up a retirement plan for the business has never been an issue because there has been no money to do it," he says. His wife, who is thirty-two, also works in the business and has very little saved for retirement.

Steve tries to economize. His last vacation was in 1990. When he bought a new car recently, it was to replace one that was seven years old and had been driven 124,000 miles. "I also get some tax benefits from the business that other people may not get, but it's not enough" to enable him to save what he needs for retirement.

Currently Steve and his wife put $2,000 each per year into IRAs. Even if he had more cash, he would not invest it in the stock market, which he says "is not sound." He hopes to build up the value of the business in order to sell it at some point.

But right now Steve thinks his most important retirement asset is his house, where he intends to continue living when and if he ever stops working. He paid 50 percent down when he bought the house in 1996, and currently he owes about $160,000. Luckily he has a source besides his lethargic business for doing this: Over the next three or four years, he expects to receive about $30,000 annually from a friend who owes him money. Steve will apply all of these funds to the mortgage, so that even if the house is not totally paid off, the monthly mortgage payment will be substantially less than it is now.

For Steve and his wife, the advantage of this plan is that it preserves several retirement options: to sell the house, move to a less expensive residence, and use the extra funds for retirement expenses; or to actually live in the house and have only a very small or no mortgage payment at all.

#29

Take Out a Reverse Mortgage That Will Provide Extra Retirement Income.

If you want to continue living in your home when you retire, the extra income from a reverse mortgage can make the difference between having a financial "cushion" and not having one. In the story that follows, Herb and Josie receive a monthly cash payment from their reverse mortgage, but there are other alternatives. If you want to pay off a debt, you may benefit most from taking the money in a lump sum. Or if your primary concern is knowing that cash will be available in an emergency, you may want to choose a line of credit that you can tap when you need it.

Herb is one of those amazingly energetic seniors. He's seventy-nine years old and still working as a house painter about fifteen to eighteen hours a week. A plainspoken midwestern man with a good sense of humor, Herb owns his own business and vows that he'll continue working "until about four days before my funeral."

In the meantime, he wants to make sure that his seventy-eight-year-old wife, Josie, will be financially secure if he should pass away before she does. Herb receives about $1,050 per month in Social Security and Josie collects about $500. They do not have any other pensions. Their main asset is the 1,100-square-foot, single-family, ranch-style home they've lived in for nearly thirty-five years. In 1998, they still owed about $13,000 on their mortgage. Herb said that for years he had been thinking about ways to leverage their home equity into some income, "possibly arranging with someone who might want to make an investment" in their house. Then he heard about reverse mortgages and started shopping around until he found the deal he thought would be most helpful financially.

Herb and Josie paid $5,000 in closing costs for the mortgage, and in return they are receiving $425 per month for the rest of their lives. When they have both passed away, the house will be sold to pay off the mortgage. They are not big spenders. "We try to be somewhat frugal. At our age we don't need a lot of things." His favorite pastimes are playing golf and reading. "Actually I could stop working and we could still live comfortably," Herb says.

To Herb and Josie, the main value of the reverse mortgage is to "have a cushion." As long as they receive the $425 a month and Herb is working, they are able to put all of Josie's Social Security in the bank each month. In the bank, where the interest earned on the savings is very low? "That's right," Herb says. But that money may not be in the bank for long. That's because, for the first time in his life—when he is not painting or playing golf or reading—under the tutelage of one of his children, Herb is learning how to invest in the stock market.

#30

Secure a Home Equity Loan to Buy Real Estate That Can Either Produce Retirement Income or Serve as a Retirement Home.

The tax deductions that you receive for payments on your own home mortgage or on a real estate property you buy for investment can be a big boon if you need to catch up on retirement savings. But before you rush to do this, just remember that there's a lot more to being a landlord or landlady than collecting the tenants' rent checks.

Jeanette is a real estate agent, so it was logical that she and her husband would invest in property to bolster their retirement resources.

For many years, "retirement didn't seem like an issue," she reflects. "But all of a sudden it's here." Jeanette's sixty and her husband, Larry, is sixty-one. He's just retired from a career as a truck driver. His Social Security income is about $10,000 a year, but currently he's supplementing that by doing part-time jobs, such as working in a friend's used car lot and occasionally driving a truck.

For many years Larry did not have any retirement benefits or savings. But when he and Jeanette were in their forties, she remembers, "we started seeing the handwriting on the wall for

our retirement—with the costs of hospitalization and inflation" looming, they knew that they had to start saving. When
Larry retired, he had saved about $160,000 in a 401(k), which
is managed by professional managers. He's going to avoid
withdrawing money from it as long as they can live comfortably without it.

Jeanette has been selling real estate for about twelve years.
Before that she worked in a variety of sales positions—once
selling restaurant equipment; another time, selling insurance.
She put $2,000 a year into an IRA while she was working, but
that's the only retirement asset she has.

Except for their home equity, of course. "Originally we
were going to sell our larger house and buy a smaller one to
live in. We have a big yard and pool and nobody wants to take
care of that stuff after a while," Jeanette says. But when the
house next door went on the market, they shifted strategies,
refinancing their home to take $50,000 of the $90,000 equity
they had in order to purchase the other house outright. When
they finish fixing up the new house, Jeanette estimates, it will
be worth about $120,000.

Then what will they do with the renovated house? Maybe
they'll move there and not have to worry about mortgage
payments as they get older. Maybe they'll rent it for the income, or they could even sell it and invest the profit. For the
moment, Jeanette and Larry don't need to do any of these
things because they both continue to work. But already
Jeanette can visualize a good use for the extra income they
could garner from buying the house next door: paying for
health insurance. Because Larry retired recently, they are covered by paying $391 per month for health insurance for both
of them under COBRA—a continuation of his employer's
plan. But eighteen months after his retirement, when the
COBRA ends, she estimates that their health insurance premium will jump about $200 a month. And that's what they'll
have to pay for a few years before either Jeanette or Larry can
qualify for Medicare at age sixty-five.

At that point, whatever savings or income they can earn from the house next door could come in very handy.

#31

Trade In Your Current Home for One That Costs Less to Maintain. Put Away the Savings for Retirement.

Sometimes it's not just the mortgage payment that puts a crimp in your wallet. Especially if you have a large house, maintenance, repairs, housecleaning, and the need to replace things like a fifteen-year-old stove or refrigerator can also take a financial toll. Moving to a smaller or newer home may reduce these expenses and provide you with extra cash for your retirement fund.

Margie, age fifty, describes herself as "a single mom who raised two kids and then needed to figure out what to do about retirement." While raising and supporting her children, both of whom have serious health problems, she worked full-time in a series of sales-related jobs for technology companies. But until about four years ago, none of her jobs produced a pension or any other type of retirement benefits. Margie did manage to put $2,000 a year into IRAs—now they're worth about $100,000—but now she is determined to catch up on her savings so that in a few years she can phase into retirement by starting a part-time business and "buying back time" to do the things she enjoys, such as travel.

You could say that Margie has a "multi-pronged" retirement strategy that involves both increasing her savings and cutting back on spending. For starters, she puts the maximum allowable tax-free contribution into her company 401(k) each year. She also takes advantage of the company's employee stock purchase plan, but limits that investment because she feels "it's not good to have too much invested where you work."

Over the years Margie has reined in her spending by driving an old Oldsmobile she bought for $3,000 at a car auction and fixed up for another $1,000, by using a "personal shopper" at a department store to help her find the most economical options for her business wardrobe, and by either selling her used clothing through a secondhand store or getting a tax deduction by donating the clothes to charity.

But the step with the most potential for boosting Margie's retirement savings was taking advantage of fifteen years of home equity: selling her large four-bedroom, two-car garage, brick suburban house and moving into a townhouse. "I realized that I was spending more time and money maintaining the house and property than seemed reasonable, especially given that my children were no longer living at home. I had a yard service that cost me $1,500 a year, a housekeeper, a handyman, and insurance bills. The oven broke and I had to get a new one, and I had to replace the carpet. I looked at the bills and thought: None of this money is going into the equity of the property."

Margie had bought her house fifteen years earlier for about $85,000, and she sold it for $224,000. With the proceeds from the sale, she put $45,000 down on her new home, spent $23,000 for a new car, and invested the remainder in the stock market. Since she paid cash and does not have a car payment, she has her employer make an automatic electronic salary deduction of $450 per month—the amount she would otherwise spend on a car payment—and invest it in a high-tech stock fund.

By the apparently simple act of selling the house, Margie staged what could potentially be a giant catch-up for her retirement savings. Now the primary challenge she faces is to make sure that her investments perform well. "I haven't devoted enough attention to learning about my finances as I should have over the years, but I hire help," Margie says.

The help comes from a financial planner who worked with Margie to set savings targets and also manages her portfolio. Two or three times a year the planner creates colored charts to illustrate Margie's progress, and "so far I'm exceeding my goals in a big way," Margie says.

What has Margie learned from her own personal race to retirement? Start saving early, and make sure that every job you take allows you to save. If you work on contracts, "you need to be savvy about your billing rate, about the profit the company is making and when you can collect your benefits." And even if you're on salary, she says, "the days when you can go to work for a company and let them say 'trust me'" to provide your retirement benefits are long past.

#32

Sell Your Current Home. Use the Proceeds to Buy an RV and See the Country.

Living in an RV can be a fun and cost-saving way to retire. If you're stymied about how to save enough in time to retire, this is a lifestyle you might want to consider. If you own your home, there's a good chance that the proceeds of selling it will more than cover the cost of an RV and the expenses associated with life on the road. This lifestyle is not everyone's cup of tea, but thousands of Americans wouldn't have their retirement any other way.

When last heard from, Ben and Millie, ages sixty-three and sixty, were in their RV headed for Mardi Gras in New Orleans. In the year or so since they'd retired, they had visited, among other places, the Upper Peninsula of Michigan; Ontario; Gettysburg, Pennsylvania; and Alabama. In June, they planned to nose their thirty-nine-foot self-contained camper into a caravan of twenty RVs for a forty-seven-day tour of New Brunswick, Nova Scotia, Labrador, and other Canadian points east.

This couple has always loved traveling. Even though the family was on a tight budget, when their three children were younger, they enjoyed piling them into the car for vacation road trips. Now that they're retired, Ben and Millie are doing what they most like to do—exploring the country, living in their RV, and when that vehicle is ensconced in a park, unhooking the car they tow behind the RV to get a closer look at local attractions.

But it was not always clear that Ben and Millie would be able to live this retirement dream. Ben had quit high school before joining the service at age eighteen. After completing his military service, getting a high school equivalency diploma, and getting married, he worked as an electronics technician for companies that had contracts to work on space exploration vehicles. The young family, however, was always struggling economically. So in his mid-forties, Ben went to college, receiving his degree as an electrical engineer when he was forty-seven. Armed with the new credentials, he was able to get a better job with a higher salary.

For many years Ben had earned no retirement benefits. He and Millie found it impossible to save any money at all, and the family had gone into debt, refinancing the house to help pay the bills. After ten years working with a Fortune 500 company, he was eligible for the pension plan. But at the beginning he was only allowed to contribute $200 a year to the account. Later on, the company started a 401(k), and most years he contributed 2 percent of his gross income to his account.

When Ben was fifty-one and the expenses of raising a family had decreased somewhat, he and Millie refinanced their house, used the cash this generated to pay off their bills and to start investing in the stock market, and took a fifteen-year mortgage. "We tried to change our lifestyle, going out a little bit more, taking vacations we couldn't afford before. But I also realized that we really needed to save more for retirement. That's when I started watching expenses carefully. For example, if I needed a new car, I compared finance charges, and I looked into whether it would make more sense to pay for it with cash or to take out a loan."

A few years later, when Ben was fifty-five, he and Millie acknowledged that while they were enjoying their new lifestyle, they may have been doing so at the expense of their retirement security. "I really began focusing on retirement when I was fifty-five," Ben says, "and I realized that I was going to be in deep trouble" financially, even if they waited until he was sixty-five to retire. But before that, they had an unexpected stroke of luck. When Ben was sixty-two, the company offered him a buyout to retire early. By then, he had saved about $200,000 in his 401(k). The company added $75,000 in cash. He was also eligible for Social Security by then.

So Ben accepted the buyout and he and Millie set out on their new life. "We had always planned on selling the house when I retired," Ben recalled, because they wanted to spend time traveling and living in an RV. They sold the house and used some of the profit to pay off the loan on the camper they owned at the time. This transaction left them with $75,000 in cash, which they entrusted to their daughter, who is a stockbroker, to manage for them.

After retiring, Ben had invested $17,000 in an online brokerage account. When the investment's value hit $45,000, he took the money out of the account and used it as a down payment for the $120,000 camper where they live now. This new home has lots of amenities—convection and microwave ovens, a full-size refrigerator, a bedroom with a queen-size bed, a bath with a shower and two television sets. "Living this way is cheaper and you have much more freedom," Ben says. As members of various camping clubs, they get discounts: on average, they pay $9 per night to park the camper at locations all over the country. Although the tab to fill the ninety-gallon gas tank can easily add up to $100, they can travel six hundred or seven hundred miles on the full tank.

When and if they get tired of life on the road, Ben and Millie will be able to apply the equity in their camper to buying a new home—one that is not on wheels. And they will also have the principal in their 401(k)—currently in investments being managed by their daughter—which they haven't even touched and don't expect to need for several years.

#33

Sell Your Expensive Home and Use the Tax-Free Profit to Finance Early Retirement.

Living in an ample house and almost unconsciously acquiring large quantities of furniture and other possessions, you can easily forget that other lifestyles are within your grasp. Sometimes all it takes to completely shift your mindset about retirement is hearing how someone else has made it work financially. The couple in this story decided to use the profits from their home to live more economically in Mexico. But they could have chosen any other inexpensive location, and the lesson they offer would still be the same.

Do you dream of retiring in your fifties, while you're still at your physical and mental prime and before you are old enough to qualify for either Social Security or Medicare? If you own your home and if you have substantial equity or its value has appreciated significantly, selling the house may be the key to realizing your dream. That's exactly what happened to Roslyn and Ray, who used to live in California, in one of the country's most expensive zip codes.

Roslyn and Ray—she's fifty-two and he's fifty-four—worked as self-employed counselors for nearly twenty years. After leaving counseling, Roslyn also worked for several years in a high-stress retail business where she had to oversee employees and manage inventory. They invested whatever money they could save from their earnings. But as residents of a high-cost area, Roslyn says, "we didn't have a clear idea of what we needed" to retire because they couldn't figure out how to escape from paying the mortgage, taxes, and upkeep for their house. Until recently, leaving behind their demanding work lives simply did not appear to be an option. "We kept dreaming of early retirement," Roslyn recalls, but "we felt caught in a cycle of work, work, work, and no end in sight."

Then in 1997 they ran into some old friends with whom they had lost contact. The friends had retired to live in Mexico at age thirty-nine, inspired by a book they read that suggested selling your home and possessions and opting for living a "simpler but better life off the growth in their capital." In an e-mail, Roslyn described the eye-opening effect of running into these old friends. "Finding out how much they [the friends] lived on clicked the switch in our heads. All we needed to do was look at the problem differently. Sell our house!"

Continuing to live in their California home, they estimated, would require a retirement budget of $44,000 per year. Instead, they were able to retire when they were fifty-one and fifty-three, respectively, on an estimated annual budget of about $24,000. How did they do it?

The first and most important step was deciding to sell their 2,100-square-foot house. They reaped a $175,000 profit—all of it free of federal taxes. With the house profit and some funds in a money market, now they are sure that they can live on these resources for several years until Ray becomes eligible for Social Security.

After touring the U. S. searching for a retirement home, they visited Lake Chapala, an area near Guadalajara, Mexico, where many American retirees live. There they invested $105,000 to buy a car and a house. Daily living expenses are economical: Insurance on their home is $230 a year, groceries cost about $160 a month, recreation and leisure—including working out in a gym and dining at restaurants—run about $100 a month. "A shampoo, haircut, and blow-dry for me," says Roslyn, "is about five dollars, and it's just as good as what I've paid $25 for in the States."

For the foreseeable future, Roslyn and Ray are delighted to make Mexico their home. "Our lives here are as full as we want them to be," she writes. "We both volunteer, participate in volleyball, walk, work out, have the luxury of time for reading, and have more social activities than we ever had all of those working years." They're pleased with the quality and low cost of dental and medical care they've needed. Excursions to the beach, staying in touch by watching CNN on cable and using the Internet, and knowing they are close enough to visit friends and family in the States are other sources of satisfaction.

"Of course, it's not paradise here, and Mexico is a developing country, with all that implies. Certainly, not everyone would be comfortable here, but for us, at this time, it is home," says Roslyn. And so far, they don't miss the house in California at all.

TIPS

 Enlist the aid of a qualified real estate professional. To search for a credentialed Senior Real Estate Specialist in your area, call:

- Senior Advantage Real Estate Council at 800-500-4564, or look up the lists on their website at http://www.seniorsrealestate.com.

 Get the information you need on reverse mortgages. If you're interested in learning about reverse mortgages, write for information from:

- Home Equity Information Center at 601 E St. N.W., Washington, D.C. 20049, or look up the website at http://www.aarp.org/hecc.home.html.

To find a housing counselor who can help you figure out if a reverse mortgage is appropriate for you, call:

- Federal Department of Housing and Urban Development at 800-569-4287, or go to their website at http://www.hudhcc.org.

- The nonprofit, independent National Reverse Mortgage Lenders Association at 202-939-1760 or go to http://www.reversemortgage.org for a list of reverse mortgage lenders.

 Let the federal government help you profit from selling your home. For more information on the $250,000 federal tax exclusion for selling your home:

- IRS Publication 523, "Selling Your Home," by calling the publications line 800-829-3676 or through the website, http://www.irs.gov.

CHAPTER SIX

LEARN HOW TO
BE A SUCCESSFUL SAVER

"Putting away money for retirement is like giving yourself a raise. It's money that gives the freedom when you
want it—and deserve it."
— *Alexis Herman, Secretary, U.S. Department of Labor*

It's a concept that is so elementary yet so hard to implement:
systematically saving some small portion of your income to
provide for your long-term future. It's a big leap from the
childish habit of putting pennies into a piggy bank to filling
out the forms that will take 6 percent out of your grown-up
salary and deposit the money into a 401(k) before you ever see
it. And it's an even bigger leap, if you work for yourself or have
a small business with unpredictable cash flow, to commit to
putting that money away every week or every month, even if
the income for that period is bottoming out.

Let's face it: Even if our parents encouraged us to do the
piggy bank thing as children, few of us received any formal financial education at home, in school or anywhere else. "The
vast majority of students ages sixteen to twenty-two have
never taken a class in personal finance, two-thirds admit they
could use a few more lessons on money management and 28
percent of students with a credit card roll over debt each
month." That's what Don Blandin, president of the American
Savings Education Council, told a congressional committee
when he testified on the results of the 1999 Youth and Money
Survey conducted by the Washington-based organization he
heads.

Many of our parents and grandparents lived through and vividly remember the Depression. This experience has made many of them savers. Because they developed the saving habit and also because of Social Security, the elderly in the United States are much better off economically now than they were several decades ago. But baby boomers and the generations that are coming behind them did not have the Depression experience. In many cases, they have matured or at least lived the last few years in a high-flying economy where they have been constantly bombarded with incentives to enjoy the little comforts of life—to say nothing of major luxuries—right now. The effects of this "spend now, save later" mentality surface in the statistics:

- According to the U.S. Commerce Department, the personal savings rate—defined as the percent of disposable income saved—has basically been zero in recent years, following a downward trend from 9 percent in 1982.

- A 1997 study by the Public Agenda foundation found that 46 percent of Americans—including people aged fifty-one to sixty-one—have saved less than $10,000 for retirement. This is an astounding figure, given that experts recommend that to live comfortably in retirement, most people require 60 to 80 percent of the annual income they received while they were still working.

- An AARP study of baby boomers concluded that "even the top 10 percent of boomers have only modest financial assets," specifically that the typical boomer had only $1,000 in assets and that only one-fifth of boomers had more than $25,000.

In light of the current state of Americans' savings, what do individuals need do to better prepare for the future? Duke Grkovic, a financial adviser based in Richmond, Virginia, of-

fers this concise, practical advice: "The best way to work toward financial independence is to save in a tax-qualified retirement account." By tax-qualified retirement account, he
means vehicles such as the 401(k) for the private sector and
similar plans for nonprofit or public sector employees, or the
IRA for individuals. While any working person or even a
nonworking spouse can get a tax deduction for saving in an
IRA, many Americans working full-time have no retirement
plan at work. And women, members of minority groups, and
employees of small business are less likely than the population
as a whole to have access to any kind of tax-qualified retirement savings at work. For example, only 20 percent of employees of businesses with one hundred or fewer workers have
the opportunity to participate in a plan at work. People in this
situation face several serious barriers to adequate retirement
savings: There's no employer contribution to their plan, they
must develop their own personal discipline or regime for saving, and, in many cases, their only tax incentive for retirement
savings comes through an IRA, for which the annual tax deduction is limited to $3,000 in 2002-2004 (or $3,500 for people who are fifty or older).

Yet even employees who are offered tax-qualified retirement plans at work often do not maximize their potential benefits. One out of five workers who could participate in a
401(k) does not do so. This is particularly shortsighted, since on
the average, employers match employee contributions up to
about 6 percent of their annual salary, which can give compounded savings a hefty boost. According to the Profit-Sharing
Council of America, in 2000, the average 401(k) contribution
was $3,651, far below the limit of $10,500. Even systematic
savers often lose their commitment to retirement savings when
they change jobs, taking out the accrued savings in a lump sum
and—instead of rolling the money over into an IRA or other
tax-qualified retirement account—spending it on other things.
The Department of Labor reported that in 1994, only 16 percent of workers under forty and 32 percent of those over forty

who received lump sums from their retirement plans put the money back into retirement savings.

Officials in Washington, D.C., have become so concerned about these signs of inadequate retirement savings that Congress passed a law requiring the government to sponsor a National Summit on Retirement Savings in 1998, to be followed by similar conferences in 2002 and 2005. One of the charges to the experts and officials who attended the conference was to examine why so many Americans are not saving enough for a comfortable retirement.

Perhaps the most prevalent answer was lack of education: As a nation, we are still woefully ignorant about the basic economics of retirement. What exactly is it that we don't know? There are lots of answers. Remember Rita (page 28) in Chapter 2? She admitted she didn't know how much even minimal savings could grow over a number of years because of compounding. To see how much compounding can make even a small amount of savings grow, consider this example: Here are the results that you could produce by saving $50 a month with an annual return of 8 percent:

- For ten years, you'd put in $6,000 and end up with $9,147.

- For twenty years, you'd put in $12,000 and end up with $29,451.

- If you continued to contribute for thirty years, you'd have put in $18,000 and the total in the account would be $74,518.

Something else that most people don't know is how much money they will need to live on when they retire. According to Public Agenda, nearly 60 percent of people say that in retirement, they expect to have the same standard of living as when they were working. Yet 71 percent did not know how much money this would require. This ignorance is confirmed by the 2001 Retirement Confidence Survey conducted by the Employee Benefit Research Institute, the American Savings Education Council, and Mathew Greenwald & Associates, which reports that only 39 percent of workers have tried to calculate how much money they will need to save for their retirement—down from 51 percent two years before.

Some of the other barriers to retirement savings identified by participants in the National Summit on Retirement Savings held in Washington in 1998 were:

- Consumerism—the public's vulnerability to a barrage of messages that promote buying rather than saving.

- The federal tax code, which penalizes earnings on retirement savings that are outside qualified plans such as 401(k)s or IRAs.

- Money saved in some plans—even though there may be penalties for early withdrawal—is too accessible to people who decide to use it for other, sometimes frivolous purposes.

- Tax-qualified plans are sometimes too complex for small employers to figure out and implement or too expensive.

- Lack of adequate income.

As mentioned in the introduction, recently Uncle Sam has put in place legislation to help break down some of these barriers. The new rules lifted limits on tax-deductible contributions to retirement plans; special, additional "catch-up" contribution limits for people age 50 and older; and the elimination of earnings penalties for Social Security recipients who are still working and are 65 or older.

Politicians are still debating what to do about the future of Social Security, which will affect almost everyone's retirement planning. But regardless of what happens to Social Security, the challenge for individuals remains the same:

How can you start—today and within the existing rules and programs—to catch up on your retirement savings? That's what the stories in this chapter are about: the Art of Saving.

34

Enroll in a Financial Planning or Money Management Course.

It's tempting to believe that we know all we need to know about managing money because, after all, we have done it all of our adult lives. Yet if ends do not meet at the end of every month, and debt is piling up and savings are nil, this could mean it's time to consider getting some formal financial education. Many community colleges and other educational institutions and organizations offer such courses on the community level. One program that offered this opportunity, known as Money 2000™, was sponsored by the Cooperative State Research, Education and Extension Service of the U.S. Department of Agriculture. This story explains how attending a Money 2000™ course helped one woman get out of debt and start saving for retirement. (At press time, the department was making plans for a similar effort called Money 2020.)

"I am fortunate that I have seen the light and I have fifteen years yet to save for retirement," says Bonnie. She's fifty-one years old and serves as an administrative assistant to a school superintendent in the Midwest. "The light" Bonnie's referring to is what she learned from Money2000™ about how to save so that she could pay off an accumulation of debts and build a retirement fund.

Bonnie had several jobs in the public and private sectors, but her retirement savings were minimal. Most of her jobs did not offer retirement benefits. At one job, she accumulated about $2,000 in a pension, but when she left, instead of rolling it over into a retirement account, Bonnie spent the money. When she was divorced, she rejected her lawyer's advice to fight for a share of her ex's pension. "My kids got involved and said: 'This is all that Dad has,'" Bonnie explains.

In 1997 Bonnie realized that "my saving habits, or lack thereof, were causing me to fall short of one of my goals, which was traveling. And being an impulse buyer certainly didn't help the situation. I loved buying gifts and making gift baskets for my friends and co-workers—which could sometimes be expensive. As I began to see my savings balance dwindle and my expenses rise, I realized I needed to something drastic. Soon." A personal friend told her about the Money2000™ course and its basic goal of helping participants save $2,000 by the year 2000, which required her to save around $112 per month at that time.

In the program, participants set personal financial goals, figure out how much they need to save to pay off their debts, and keep track of how well they're sticking to their plans. Bonnie has several goals: to pay off her credit card debt (some of it with interest rates as high as 22 percent) and loans, to buy a condo to live in so she can stop paying rent, to travel, and to have enough money set aside for a comfortable retirement.

Bonnie's money plan requires her to put about $100 per month into the retirement plan at work. But she just got a 3.75 percent raise, and she plans either to save an additional $150 per month in the retirement account or to start using some of the raise to invest in stocks. Whatever she can save for retirement will be supplemented by about $850 that she'll eventually receive each month from Social Security. In addition, her car loan will soon be paid off, and then she'll apply that same amount of money to saving to buy a condo.

The system is definitely working for Bonnie, who as a result of taking the money management course has a whole new attitude about her money and her future. Learning "how little money Americans are saving for retirement made me look at it a lot harder," Bonnie says. "Now, I know I am doing something," she says, and if she can stick to the savings plan, she'll be poised for exactly the retirement life that she wants to have.

#35

Resist the Temptation to Sacrifice Your Retirement Savings to Immediate Needs for Cash.

When bills are piling up, the money "sitting" in a 401(k) or an IRA or any other type of retirement account can emit a siren's song that's hard to resist. Why not just take out a little here or there to paint the house or take a nice vacation or pay for your daughter's wedding? The answer is simple: Because the money will not be there when you need it to retire. That sum and the amount of money you'd earn from compounding can never really be replaced.

Paula's fifty-five now, and she's recently become very aware of all the retirement savings she could have had. Almost every time she'd accumulated some money that could be used for retirement, she ended up spending it on something else.

After finishing college, already married, Paula spent the first five years of her career as a schoolteacher. When she and her husband uprooted themselves from the East Coast to live "closer to nature" in a western state, "I did a really dumb thing," she admits. "I cashed in my retirement money and bought a couch. I thought I had lots of time" before she needed to think about retirement. Actually, the total retirement fund was around $5,000, so it paid for more than a couch—some current expenses and some money for savings, although these were not earmarked for retirement and did not go into an IRA, where she could have avoided paying taxes on it. That $5,000, if invested at a 6 percent return, would have been worth nearly $16,000 in twenty years, or close to $29,000 in thirty years.

Happily ensconced with her husband and young daughter in a woodsy environment, Paula taught for about five years at a local college that had a state pension system. Then her marriage broke up, they sold the house, and she moved back to the East Coast. And once again, when she left the teaching job, she cashed out the pension fund, which was worth about $4,000. Now supporting two children on her own, she worked for two years at another college position that did not give her any retirement benefits or savings. "I was the major support for my children and I had to make more money. At that time, pensions and retirement were not at all on my mind," she explains. After two years, she left for a better job with a retirement plan on a different campus. Paula remained in this job for nine years, during which she met her second husband. She has not cashed out this pension. It will generate about $9,000 a year in income for her once she turns sixty-two. The only other retirement income she can count on at the moment is Social Security—$680 per month at age sixty-two, about $900 at sixty-five, and $1,190 if she starts at age seventy.

A few years after their marriage, Paula and her second husband moved to a small town some distance from the college where they had both been working. Their home has a wonderful view of woods and river, but the house needed major work, so they ended up using "lots of SEPs and IRAs" that her husband had put away to pay for the cost of a major addition and renovation. After many years of working in public relations in academia, Paula made another life-changing decision: to enroll in a seminary and become a minister. It took more than seven years of mostly part-time attendance, with a grueling schedule and academic challenges that included learning Greek and Hebrew, but now she's finished and on the road to becoming an ordained minister—who eventually will receive not only a salary, but also some health insurance and retirement benefits. And this time she plans to save the retirement benefits for retirement.

#36

As Your Income Increases, Put More Money into Retirement Accounts.

It's tempting to view a salary increase as "free" money to spend on an immediate need or a whim. However, if you have not reached your retirement savings goals, one lesson that can serve you well is to dedicate at least a portion of the increase to securing your future.

Fred, fifty-two, and Joan, fifty, are both teachers, so it's not hard to understand that for many years they put all the money they could save into a fund for their two children's college education. The wake-up call that changed their priorities came ten years ago when Fred was forty-two. "I am a teacher, not a financial person," he explains. "My brother was looking at my taxes for that year and he took an interest in my retirement. I still remember what he said to me: 'I'm looking at your finances and you aren't doing anything for your future. At this rate, you can't retire.'"

For about fifteen years before that conversation, Fred could have put money into a 403(b), a tax-deferred retirement fund, through his employment, but he had never done it. "I could give you many excuses," he says. "But none are acceptable. I guess I was always going to do it next year." Fred's response to his brother was to open a 403(b) and start saving systematically for retirement. For many years Joan worked at home raising their children. But seven years ago she went back to teaching and also started to save in a 403(b).

With no matching contributions from their employers, Fred and Joan have managed to increase their retirement funds to $245,000. A key to this growth was increasing their retirement contributions every time they got a raise. "Pay increases are usually 3 percent, although a few times they have been 15 percent. If I or my wife got a $2,000 raise, we would put 80 percent into the 403(b). On the other hand, if I only got a raise of $800, I would only save about 50 percent of that. The maximum I can contribute now is $10,000 in a year, and for my wife it is $8,000." One way they can afford this is by cutting back on routine expenses. They eat brown-bag lunches, bring their own coffee to work, and drive older cars.

Fred and Joan live in a rural area in a state in the Northeast. "We bought our home in 1976 and never wanted to move. Where we live is perfect," he says, partly because they are close enough to make short visits to several major cities.

But although they'd like to do some traveling and to be able to afford to dine out occasionally when they retire, they have no interest in moving to a high-cost urban environment. As a result, they're optimistic about being able to retire when they're sixty-two. At that point they'll start collecting Social Security, and because they will continue to increase contributions to their retirement funds, Fred says that they expect to exit from work entirely and enjoy "our home and each other."

#37

Max Out Contributions to All of Your Eligible Tax-Deferred Retirement Savings.

If your employer doesn't offer a 401(k) or some other type of tax-qualified account, then at least try to make a commitment to saving in an Individual Retirement Account or a Simplified Employee Pension, which is an IRA for people who are self-employed. Any money you put into those accounts will contribute to your financial independence in two ways: by saving you some federal taxes in the current year (unless you choose a Roth IRA, which allows you to deduct the income when you take it out, instead of the contributions when you put them in) and by ensuring that you have assets that will grow and benefit from compound interest. People whose employer automatically contributes to their retirement account are fortunate in that they do not have to shoulder the entire burden themselves. In contrast, people who are self-employed or have a small business often find themselves putting all of their income back into the business, and little or none of it into a retirement fund. This story tells of one couple's struggle to balance three financial priorities—keeping the business profitable, paying for their children's education, and saving for retirement.

Georgia, fifty-four, and Kurt, fifty-six, feel as if they are constantly working. Twenty-two years ago Georgia became a wholesale sales representative for handicrafts. After thirteen years of teaching, her husband left his job to join her as an employee of the business. They spent the retirement savings he'd accumulated from teaching to buy a house. Georgia says "our income is pathetic compared to the number of hours my husband and I are investing in it. I put in ten to fourteen hours a day on average. Sometimes I do that right through the weekends. My husband is constantly on the road. An average day of travel for him is two hundred fifty miles." Hiring additional personnel, of course, would detract from their cash flow as well as from accumulating retirement savings.

But it's not just the constant work that makes them feel battered. It's the financial hoops they jumped through to pay for several years of prep school and college for each of their two children. "The biggest mistake we made was saving for their education," Georgia says. "The schools took every bit we had saved." They realized too late that if they had not saved so much for the children's education, their kids would have been eligible to receive more financial aid, which would have put less pressure on the parents' resources.

Despite the other demands on their time and their money,

however, Georgia and Kurt have been doing something right: As long as the children were in school, they at least put money into IRAs. And when the children had finished their education, they began "squeezing out a full 15 percent of my husband's salary and a full 13 percent of mine, putting that away religiously every year" in SEPs. "We haven't been doing anything more than that, and I don't think it's enough," Georgia says. Although Georgia's disappointed in the return they've had on investments in these accounts, they have about $300,000 saved. Georgia expects to receive about $150,000 from her mother's estate soon, so recently the couple went for the first time to consult with a financial planner. Georgia wants the planner to help them figure out "where we are right now" in terms of their needs for retirement and to stimulate a discussion about what to do with their business in the future and how they actually want to spend their next few decades.

#38

Make Your Inheritance Last as Long as You'll Need It.

Not everyone has the good fortune to receive a substantial inheritance. And if an inheritance materializes, of course it could be tempting to spend the money immediately on pent-up demand for things like cars, vacations, or a new house. Instead, if you do come into a significant sum of money or property, try to develop a plan for enhancing not just your current life, but also your retirement years.

Lawrence was in his fifties. He was getting tired of working as a psychological counselor. Throughout his career he had never saved for retirement. He knew that one day he would inherit the family farm. When his father died in his eighties, Lawrence became the owner of the property his family had owned for generations. After it was sold, he had about $1 million, which he viewed as his safety net for a long-term future.

Like most of us, Lawrence had a list of items he wanted to buy immediately, including an expensive car and a piano. However, to make sure he didn't squander the inheritance, he went to a financial adviser and they created a plan: First, Lawrence would get $200,000 outright to buy the things he wanted right away. The rest of the inheritance would be invested, but each year he would spend some of the money to live. At the rates assumed by the financial planner, Lawrence's money would not run out until he was ninety-four years old.

Now Lawrence still works part-time as a counselor. Since receiving his inheritance and working out a plan for future, he has developed more confidence in his own professional value and started charging higher fees. With the higher fees and some income from the inheritance, Lawrence has been able to free up time to start on the path toward the future that he's been waiting for—devoting a substantial part of his time to creative activities, including music and art.

TIPS

 Look into taking a course that will help you manage your money and develop a savings plan. Here are some places to start:

- The community college, local college, or university or the local school system's adult education program.

- A brokerage house or other financial services company. Many of these offer brief seminars on topics such as IRAs or what to do if you receive an inheritance. Just remember that you do not have to purchase their services if you attend one of these courses.

- The U.S Department of Agriculture's Money2000™ program. You can look up information on a program in your state on the Internet at www.Money2000.org.

 Use Internet resources to calculate how your savings can grow. You can explore the many retirement planning tools by using a metasearch engine such as http://www.ask.com and looking for "retirement planning" or "retirement calculators." Or start with these websites:

- http://www.quicken.com/retirement

- http://www.investorguide.com/retirecalculators.html

 Become informed by using free government materials. Order these and other free publications from the Labor Department's toll-free information line, 800-998-7542:

- "Ten Ways to Beat the Clock and Prepare for Retirement"; "Women and Pensions: What Women Need to Know"; and "Power to Choose." You can also read these publications on the Internet at http://www.dol.gov/dol/pwba/public/pubs/main.htm and http://www.asec.org

CHAPTER SEVEN

LEARN HOW TO BE A SUCCESSFUL INVESTOR

Many experts argue that if you're saving for retirement, it's a no-brainer to put your money in the stock market, because over the long term, the market generates higher returns than just about any other use of your money.

And Americans, whether they are consciously planning for their retirement or just using up the money left over after they've paid their bills, seem to be buying into this belief in a big way. According to a study by the Investment Company Institute and the Securities Industry Association, in late 1999 "an estimated 49.2 million U.S. households, or 48.2 percent, own equities either in mutual funds or individually. Thirty-two percent own equities through employer-sponsored retirement funds, and 36 percent own equities outside such plans."

Some of the forces that have driven so many Americans to invest in the stock market are:

- The decrease in the number of defined benefit pension plans in which the employer is responsible for investing and managing the retirement fund.

- The increase in the number of defined contribution pension plans—401(k)s and other plans sponsored by companies and nonprofit or public employers— that offer employees a selection of investment options.

- The momentum of the bull market and strong economy of the 1990s.

Yet investing in the stock market—even if you commit to holding a stock for a decade—is not a sure shot for anyone. Whether you really will benefit more from buying the stock than you would from investing in real estate that may be grabbed up by developers depends on a series of factors that vary with each investor and each purchase: the amount paid for the stock, the length of time it is held, when it is sold and at what price, along with other factors.

When the final figures came in, the national stock indexes had achieved tremendous gains in the last few years of the twentieth century. However, the gains were very uneven— virtually astronomical in high-tech stocks and plodding at best in some other sectors. And the dramatic ups and downs of the markets, referred to as volatility, also signaled a warning to individual investors that no one—not even the experts—can be absolutely sure that at the moment when they need to sell it, the stock they've bought will reward them with pleasing profits.

At the same time the stock market was on a roll, trading became more accessible to the public than ever before through the Internet. Now almost anyone can open an account, monitor it and trade stocks or bonds, mutual funds, or even options, simply by a click of a mouse. In mid-1999, according to U.S. Bancorp's Piper Jaffray, there were 9.7 million online brokerage accounts, up 84 percent in just one year.

However, a recent survey of 3,000 financial planners suggests that despite their broad participation in the market, Americans may not be as knowledgeable as they should be about how to invest wisely. On a scale of 1 to 4, with 1 representing "not knowledgeable" and 4 representing "very knowledgeable," the planners rated their clients at 2.2—on the average only slightly knowledgeable—about investment issues and strategies. They gave clients' knowledge the highest rating on basic budgeting, 2.7, and the lowest, 1.6, on estate planning issues. In the same study, "retirement planning" and "investment and asset growth" were the first and the third most common client financial concerns on a list of ten.

PROTECTING YOUR INVESTMENTS

Whether to invest in the markets, how much to invest, and how actively you participate are all personal decisions that you must make based on your interest and your degree of risk tolerance. If you want to start investing or become more active in the stock market, you can work toward these goals either with or without the professional help of a broker or other financial adviser. With the Internet and discount brokerage houses, it has become easier than ever to buy and sell stocks at a relatively low price without ever dealing with a middleman such as a broker. But even if you do entrust your money to a broker or other financial adviser, you should protect your own interests by taking some time to learn how the markets work and about the basic principles of investing.

There are lots of ways you can educate yourself, most of which do not require you to invest any money at all while you're still learning. The one strategy that can cost money is joining an investment club where members contribute monthly—say, $25—to a joint portfolio. You can also take short courses in investing—usually offered in the evening—at a local college or university or sign up for seminars offered to clients and potential clients by many brokerage houses and other financial services companies. Reading financial publications, paying more attention to the business section of your newspaper, or watching television shows in which experts debate investment issues can also be helpful.

To get a feeling for the pace of the market and how the daily flow of news affects stock prices, set up the headlines page of your Internet browser (such as Microsoft Excite,

Yahoo!Finance, and others) to flash you the business news and top stories of the day every time you dial up on the Internet. On that same page you can set up a simulated stock portfolio that will reflect the minute-by-minute changes in prices of stocks that you want to watch. Even if you don't ever act on this information, or only do so occasionally, you will become more attuned to trends in the market.

Once you are comfortable with the jargon, the procedures for investing, and how to find and analyze information that can help you make investment decisions, you'll be in a better position to discuss these decisions directly with a professional, or to make informed decisions about whether to accept the views of the experts whose views seem to be aired constantly by the newspapers, magazines, and television, and online.

Federal and state laws regulate the qualifications of brokers and others who execute transactions in the market on behalf of customers, as well as the information that must be disclosed about publicly traded stocks and mutual funds. Virtually all of these laws and procedures predate the widespread use of the Internet.

Late in 1999 two major legal authorities—the federal Securities and Exchange Commission and the attorney general of New York State—issued reports recommending new procedures and rules to protect investors who are using the Internet. Among the concerns they raised were privacy issues, the need to provide investors with adequate disclosure about the risks of online trading, and the impact of technical problems—such as slow execution of orders—on consumers. The attorney general especially warned that "while online discussion forums may educate and provide a sense of community to investors, they may also provide a venue for fraudulent behavior." Examples of this could be spurious "tips" or "news" circulated by people who will benefit from other investors' decisions to buy or sell a particular stock.

A Broader Concept of Investment

In the last few years, if someone said "invest," you probably assumed they were talking about participating in the stock market. Yet buying and selling equities is by no means the only way you can invest to catch up on your retirement savings. In addition to individual stocks, there are many other financial vehicles such as mutual funds, bonds, even savings accounts, money market funds, or Certificates of Deposit.

But, as we'll see in the examples in this chapter, if you want to be creative, you can also find other profitable ways to invest for your retirement—including building up your business and buying real estate.

"Investing," after all, means using whatever assets you have to create more wealth. So if your goal is to catch up for retirement, consider the best way to make the most of all of your assets—not just of your cash.

#39

Join an Investment Club and Act on What You Learn.

Although more Americans than ever hold invest-ments in the stock market, not everyone fully knows or understands how to choose stocks or to make de-cisions about when to buy and when to sell. Many newer investors get around this issue by simply buy-ing mutual funds—often within a retirement ac-count that offers them a limited number of choices. However, if you want to learn more about investing in individual stocks, joining a club is a relatively nonthreatening, low-risk way to increase both your knowledge and your self-confidence. The National Association of Investors Corporation (NAIC) offers a support system for people who want to participate in investment clubs. Club members make a monthly contribution—for example, $30—to a joint account and use it to buy and sell stocks based on their own research and analysis. The organization provides ac-cess to a wide range of educational materials, soft-ware, and a monthly magazine to help you learn how to analyze stocks and choose which ones to buy, as well as how to purchase stocks for your own account for a low commission. (See "Tips" for infor-mation on how to contact NAIC and start a club.)

About six years ago, Deanna and several of her friends were in the age range of forty-three to fifty-three. Deanna worked as a technician in an industrial factory and also sold real estate on the side. She and her colleagues at work knew that they would receive a pension when they retired. But they also knew that their pensions would be less than their salaries. Deanna, for example, would receive about 60 percent of her former income; and in ten or fifteen years the pension alone "would not support the type of lifestyle we were accustomed to," she explains. "So we decided to start an investment club, pool our money, and start studying stocks. Then when we retired we would be better off financially, able to continue some of our lifestyle."

With the specific goal of adding to their retirement resources, the club started with five members and grew to seven. Meeting once a month, "we started studying stocks, going to classes, reading books on stock selection." Each member puts $50 per month into the club portfolio. All decisions about whether to buy or sell a stock are put to a vote. "The stock club will be an excellent way to supplement a pension," Deanna says. "We should have done it earlier." After five years, their account is worth about $33,000. The value of the time she's invested in the club, however, is even greater: What she learns through the group experience, Deanna applies to her own personal investing.

#40

Make a Commitment to Investing Systematically.

There are a lot of good reasons for not investing your savings in stocks or bonds or mutual funds. Maybe you don't fully understand how these investments work, or you don't like to take any risks, or you simply haven't felt you have enough money. Or maybe you are just busy, and don't want to take the time to keep track of an investment portfolio.

But then something happens, and you start worrying about your retirement income. For some people, the most comfortable "catch-up" strategy may be putting more money in a savings account or buying real estate that will produce income in the future. For others, the wake-up call spurs them to invest in the markets. Here's the story of one man who had dipped his toe into the investment waters, but had not made a commitment to systematic investing until one day he received a notice in the mail.

"I realized that if I didn't do something, I was going to retire as a street person. It was time to take charge of my life," admits Roger. At age fifty-three, Roger had spent twenty-five years writing, ghostwriting, editing, and publishing, but the one thing he'd never written was a retirement plan.

Now, a few years later, Roger no longer worries about becoming a street person. Instead, he dreams about the fantasy he is sure will come true: retiring in twelve years, living in a house with no mortgage, taking an international trip of two or three weeks each year, and reaping the benefits of his other retirement investment—"a significant cellar of high quality wines." The only thing that could endanger achievement of that dream now, he says, is a catastrophic downward shift in the stock market.

Here is his story: Roger is self-employed and his wife is a caseworker for international adoptions. Neither one could look forward to a pension or other retirement benefits from any jobs. "One day I got something from a financial planner in the junk mail," he recalls. That was the wake-up call. He contacted the planner and arranged for what turned out to be the first of five productive meetings. "The whole process cost $500. He came to the house three times to gather financial data. The fourth time, he had a rough master plan for our financial lives. The fifth time he actually had the plan," Roger recalls.

Roger had previously been studying stock and bond funds and he had some money in mutual funds. But "the single greatest value of the entire planning process was to establish how many dollars we needed to retire comfortably and how fast we had to fund the investment vehicles." When investing for retirement, Roger concluded, "the only things that count are the time the money is invested, the amount invested per month, and the return on the investment. Those things determine whether you'll have enough to spend when you are old."

Roger did not want to devote a lot of time to managing a portfolio. From his research, he identified an index fund that had performed well over several decades and chose that as his retirement savings vehicle. Roger reviews the progress of the fund about once a year. In the meantime, he and his wife have stuck to their plan, investing a specific amount each month that he is confident will add up to the funds they will need when it is time to retire.

#41

Pay More Attention to Your Investments.

Millions of people now have IRAs and 401(k)s, but are still passive investors. Once they have made their annual IRA selection or chosen a mutual fund or two for their 401(k), people who are not accustomed to investing often don't pay attention to this money. Many people interviewed for this book did not know what their returns were on these accounts or could not even describe the investments accurately. One way to play catch-up on retirement savings is to take a more active role in trying to maximize those investments.

"I had about $60,000 in my IRA and I began to get scared," recalls Becky. That was about five years ago when she was forty-one. Since then, this self-employed graphics designer has paid more and more attention to what's going on with her retirement savings, and her strategy is paying off.

Before becoming self-employed, Becky worked for several companies. She put $2,000 a year into IRAs and accumulated some relatively small amounts in 401(k)s. At age thirty-six she married George, a civil servant who was struggling to pay off debts for his graduate education. In the early years of their marriage, their energy was focused on their two young children, and "it took us a few years to stop being separate about money," she says. "But now we are both saving for the two of us."

Becky's strategy has been to educate herself about the stock market and use the information she gleans to make considered decisions about how to invest her retirement savings. When she began to focus on investing a few years ago, she started learning by reading "money magazines." But as Internet resources have expanded, she says, "I find the Internet my best source for financial information. I look to morningstar.com, Yahoo! Finance, and street.com for information and articles, and I follow the chat boards on my holdings to get a sense of the community that I'm part of."

This does not mean, however, that Becky spends a lot of money on stock trades. When she decided to take control of her portfolio, she moved all of the retirement accounts to one major financial services company that sends her one statement a month. "I wanted as much growth as possible with minimum risk, so I created a portfolio of mostly blue chip stocks in funds and some small caps [which she later sold so she could put more money into more aggressive tech funds] to balance it out." Becky owns no individual stocks, only mutual funds, and currently most of her money is in tech funds. "Anyone that's creating hardware or laying cable is where I want to be.... That's where the growth will be for the short term, I believe."

Becky checks the status of her mutual funds daily but she doesn't buy or sell very often. "I think of my tech mutual funds as stocks and that makes me feel like a financial wheeler-dealer while I do nothing but hold them," she says.

So far Becky's approach is working. "I'm a girl who saves beyond my means," she observes. When you're self-employed, though, the limit on your annual contribution to your tax-deferred Simplified Employee Pension depends on your income, and that can be hard to predict. Last year Becky was so good at saving in her SEP, that when her income totals came in at the end of the year, she'd exceeded her allowable limit and actually had to take money out.

But that's only a temporary setback. Becky's retirement stash is up to nearly $120,000, and she's already starting to dream about the lifestyle her investments might support in the future: "I'd like to retire around sixty with enough money to travel without worry, living in different places throughout the year . . . maybe by season. Fall in Europe, summer in the U.S., and winter someplace warm."

#42

Invest in
Building Up Your Business.

We live in a very entrepreneurial era. On the grand scale, we see the high-tech and Internet businesses whose names, in the course of a few months, become household words. On a more local, personal level, all around us, we see people who are starting businesses, working for themselves and/or working out of their own homes. People who work in small businesses—especially what you might call micro-businesses, with one or a handful of employees—may find saving for retirement can be a big challenge. If you have employees, in order to set up your own tax-qualified retirement plan, you must also provide one for the people who work for you. A new or micro-business often cannot afford this. Also, for a tiny new enterprise, financial survival may depend on putting every penny of the proceeds back into the business.

In these cases, the owner's retirement savings are not in stocks or bonds: they are an investment in building the business.

Ruth was not even forty years old yet when she went to a financial planner to figure out how to catch up on saving for retirement. This talented, creative woman had established an interior design business. She liked the work, but already she knew that her goal was "by age fifty-five, to walk away from it," and to have $4,500 per month to live on.

When she first met with the planner, Ruth had no retirement savings and her business was struggling with substantial debt. The planner became her business as well as her personal financial adviser. The first step was strategizing about how to make the business more financially successful. After he helped her realize that communication was a key to business success, she enrolled in a course that helped her polish her skills in dealing with clients and potential clients. He also encouraged her to be more aggressive about finding customers by joining professional associations and by getting to know real estate agents who would be aware of new office buildings whose owners might need her services.

These steps were really part of a retirement plan: If Ruth could increase the value of her business, in the future, she would be able to sell it for a higher price, therefore increasing her personal wealth.

Following a complete financial analysis of the business,

Ruth took several steps that are also leading her to financial independence. One step was a plan for paying off her debt. Another was setting up retirement savings plans—a 401(k) plan and profit-sharing for herself and her employees. At the beginning, she put $3,000 or $4,000 per year into her own account. As her business improved, she contributed more money—at first about $10,000 and finally $25,000, per year. Now Ruth's business is so successful that she's implementing the next stage of her roadmap to financial independence: putting the profit that she cannot save in tax-qualified plans into a separate personal investment account.

Ruth is now actually ahead of her own planning. If she wants to "walk away" at age fifty-one instead of age fifty-five, she'll take with her about a million dollars in savings, plus whatever proceeds she receives from selling her interest in the business.

#43

Invest in Real Estate.

Buying an apartment, a house, or a commercial building and becoming a landlord or landlady is not to everyone's taste. But for someone who doesn't mind managing property, or whose business acumen enables him or her to make a good investment and/or hire a manager, real estate investment can be a viable route to increasing retirement savings or income. This story shows how investing in real estate has become an integral part of one woman's vision of her retirement lifestyle.

You might say that until she got into real estate, Alison was a passive investor. She is an artist, fifty-six years old and single, who has spent most of her career working in academia. While teaching, she has been building up two retirement accounts with TIAA-CREF. Trying to remember exactly what investments she had and what the rules governing those accounts are, Alison admitted that she was "foggy" about the details. "I don't have anyone close to me who can advise me, anyone I want to tell my financial situation to," she said. She credits a mentor, an older woman who teaches at the same college, with encouraging her to contribute 5 percent of her salary every year to the retirement accounts so that she could bene-fit from the match contributed by the institution.

With some money in stocks and some in bonds, thanks to the booming market of the late 1990s, she's accrued about $160,000 in retirement savings without actively managing the money.

When her mother died a couple of years ago, Alison in-herited about $125,000 in stock. She left some of the inheri-tance in the original investments, but she also decided to take a step to become a more active investor: Along with a sister, Alison contributed "a chunk" of the money to purchase a two-bedroom chalet on a woodsy mountainside in a popular retirement area in North Carolina. "We wanted to get some money into an investment that was not stocks. Since we planned to move to the state when we retire, we thought we should invest there so that we could manage it ourselves." The two sisters have also invested in property for themselves—for their own future homes—in the same area.

Although she's tired of the rigors of academia and psycho-logically ready to retire now and concentrate on her own art-work, Alison plans to stay on the college faculty at least until she's fifty-nine and a half. This will increase her pension and enable her to avoid paying penalties on withdrawals from her retirement accounts. In the meantime, the sisters have rented out the house in the woods for $800 per month. Since they don't live in the area yet, they pay for a professional rental manager, but they clear over $100 per month from the rental.

Whenever Alison does leave academia, she knows that in addition to the TIAA-CREF accounts and her Social Security, she'll be able to get some income from the rental property, which, she hopes, will also increase in value over the years.

TIPS

 Join an investment club. For information about how to start or join an investment club, contact:

- The National Association of Investors Corporation by calling their toll-free line at 877-275-6242, or by looking up their website at http://www.better-investing.org.

 Become savvy about consumer investment issues. For tips on numerous consumer issues such as how to choose a broker or how to spot investment frauds, contact:

- The Securities and Exchange Commission, a federal agency. The website, at http://www.sec.gov, has a wealth of guidance on investing under the "investor education" category. You can read many useful publications online by clicking on "Investor Education" on the home page, then on "Learning" and on "Publications." You can order print copies of publications such as "Get the Facts on Saving and Investing" and "Invest Wisely," a guide to mutual funds, by calling the SEC's toll-free number, 800-SEC-0330.

- The North American Securities Administrators Association, which represents officials who regulate the securities industry on the state level. At their site, www.nasaa.org, you can find out what agency in your state is responsible for monitoring brokers and other financial services, as well as read publications on such topics as how to watch out for dishonest investment advisers. To get printed materials, call the organization at 202-737-0900.

Consider the various online investment opportunities. If you want to explore options for investing online, these websites can help you sort through the more than 150 online brokerages:

- http://www.forrester.com, which ranks the top five "power brokers"

- http://www.gomezadvisors.com, which will help you decide what type of brokerage services you need and provides rankings of the top twenty brokerages for different types of investors

- http://www. sonic.net/donaldj/brokers.html for rankings of the top discount brokers

 Use the Internet sites to learn more about investing, real estate, and small businesses. Informative sites for learning about how to invest:

- http://www.investorguide.com

- http://www.investoreducation.org, for the Investor Education Alliance

For the basics on how mutual funds work:

- http://www.mfea.com, for the Mutual Fund Education Alliance

For educating yourself about options trading:

- http://www.cboe.com, for the Chicago Board Options Exchange site

Basic information on investing in real estate is available from these two sites:

- http://www.realtor.com, which includes a "library section" with a glossary of real estate terms and Fre-

quently Asked Questions on buying and selling a
home.

- http://www.realestate.com, which will help you analyze the investment prospects of a property you may
be interested in buying.

For help with building a small business and other related
matters, in addition to finding an individual financial adviser, you should contact:

- The federal government's Small Business Administration at http://www.sba.gov, or by calling toll-free to
800-827-5722. This agency offers free one-to-one
counseling, as well as technical assistance and numerous educational programs, available all over the
country.

CHAPTER EIGHT

MOVE TO A
LESS EXPENSIVE LOCATION

Whether you are still in the retirement planning phase or are already retired, one answer to the problem of making the most of your limited savings may be to relocate to an area with a lower cost of living.

"Relocating" does not necessarily mean that you have to move hundreds or thousands of miles from your current home. Sometimes just moving out of the city into an adjacent suburb or small town can lessen the cost of keeping a roof over your head.

In fact, most people who are fifty or older prefer to continue to live in the same home when they retire. This has been confirmed consistently by several surveys conducted by the AARP over more than a decade. The most recent is the 1996 survey, "Understanding Senior Housing: Into the Next Century—Survey of Consumer Preferences, Concerns and Needs." In the 1996 survey, 83 percent of the 1,300 people over fifty who were asked by AARP said they agreed with the statement: "What I'd really like to do is stay in my own home and never move."

But another, more recent study suggests that younger Americans are more likely to include changing their residence in their retirement plans. The 1998 Fannie Mae National Housing Survey, which focused on baby boomers, generation Xers, and homeownership, found that about one-third of Americans aged forty to fifty-four expect to move when they retire; as many as 39 percent of those aged twenty-five to thirty-nine.

There can be many motivations for moving to another location when you retire: living in a warmer climate, having easy access to the grandchildren or other family, and even the spirit of adventure that propels some American retirees to collect their Social Security payments in such far-flung locations as Australia or Brazil. According to the Social Security Administration, at the end of 1998, more than 214,000 Americans were receiving their retirement checks in more than fifty different countries.

But another, less discretionary motivation for choosing a new home for retirement may be financial, because most people must live on less income after they retire than when they were working. About a third of the empty nesters—parents whose children no longer reside with them—participating in the Fannie Mae survey said that they expected to buy a less expensive home for retirement than the one where they lived with their children.

Even if you've paid off your mortgage, the cost of utility bills, repairs, and other maintenance on your home when you stop working may be prohibitive. Furthermore, there is a severe shortage in this country of what is called "affordable" housing—rental units available to older, low-income retirees. The federal government reports that nearly three-quarters of retirees who live at or below the poverty level are paying more than 30 percent of that minimal income for rent.

What you pay in rent or a mortgage payment, of course, represents only a fraction of what you need to spend on a regular basis. So to get a true picture of the cost of living in a particular location, you have to examine many other factors. If you live in the north in the United States or in Canada, the cost of winter heating bills may be significant. This expense prompts some retirees to become "snowbirds," living several months each year in a warmer climate and returning to the north for the summer months. Residing in a small town or in the country instead of in a city may make a big difference in the cost of everything from dinner in a restaurant to going to the movies.

One of the biggest potential bites in a retirement budget is taxes of all kinds. These can vary tremendously depending on where you live. A 1994 survey by the National Conference of State Legislators found that most states provided some type of tax relief for senior citizens. At that time, thirty-five states excluded some portion of—but not necessarily all—pension income from state income taxes. Some states are particularly generous to retired civil servants or military personnel. Other benefits offered by some states include a higher standard deduction for senior citizens or exclusion of some income received from investments. And as some of the people whose stories are told in this chapter have found out, moving to a location with lower property taxes can make a significant difference in the lifestyle of retirees who depend on a fixed income.

Future retirees looking for a more economical place to live in the U.S. may actually have an advantage over current retirees who are ensconced and don't want to relocate. That's because a number of states have mounted campaigns—including tax breaks—to lure retirees to become residents. The primary motive of these states is to reap economic benefits from retirees, who usually bring assets with them, buy real estate, and generally contribute to the flow of money into the economy—without adding significantly to expenses for infrastructure such as schools and roads.

The advantage to the retiree is the opportunity to live better on a lower budget. Several of these recruiting states are in the South, where the cost of living often lags behind the national average. Mississippi, for example, operates the "Hometown Mississippi" program, which certifies more than twenty communities as "retirement cities" based on what it costs to live there. In scoring the communities, Hometown Mississippi considers expenses such as health care, real estate, and transportation.

Douglas Gray, author of *The Canadian Snowbird Guide*, describes how some Canadians may achieve financial savings—or at least improve their lifestyle with no additional cost—by spending the summer months up north and the colder months in places such as Florida, Arizona, or Texas. For example, if you sell a larger home and buy a less expensive apartment up north, you can use the extra funds to live in a mobile home during the winter. "You can buy a mobile home for around $5,000 at the end of the winter season," Gray says, "and for a pad to park it on, you pay about $150 to $300 per month, depending on how luxurious the mobile home park is, whether you are there or not. The only cost for the winter months when you are not using the home is the pad, which is less than a mortgage for a larger house would cost." He also points out that states that are popular with snowbirds are "farmers' markets," where you can buy high-quality local fruit and vegetables for much less than they would cost in climates to which they have to be transported.

If you see that your retirement savings are not going to support—or currently don't support—the lifestyle you want in your current location, that could be tip-off to consider a change. No immediate commitment is required. Like some of the people whose experiences are recounted in this chapter, you should devote some time—such as pre-retirement vacations—to exploring the options before making a decision. Thus even if moving was not what you originally had in mind for your retirement, it's a strategy that could provide you with new friends and a new way of life—as well as release the daily pressure on your retirement budget.

If you do decide to investigate other locations, make a checklist of the costs you want to compare. Make sure it includes the following: rent or mortgage, utilities, transportation, taxes, health care, and entertainment such as dining out or, if you're an avid golfer, greens fees.

#44

Compare Overall Costs of Living in Your Current Location with the Costs of Living Elsewhere.

Chapter 4 described how you can analyze your current expenses and income as a basis for creating a realistic retirement budget. Once you have done that analysis, you'll have a basis for comparing costs in your current location with other places you might choose to live.

"Gary said that finding a place to retire was harder than starting out when we were first married," says Jackie with a laugh. That's because they devoted about three years to a thorough, systematic search for the perfect retirement location—a place that offered lots of amenities at an affordable price.

This couple spent most of their life in northern states, including Ohio and New Jersey. Gary had several different jobs in the private sector and with a college that offered some retirement benefits; Jackie operated a bed-and-breakfast in their home. "But we also had four kids," Gary explains, "so for many years there wasn't much left over to save for retirement. That's why we wanted to look for a place that would match our assets."

They began their search for a retirement spot by taking a long vacation starting in South Carolina and exploring possible locations all the way north to Maine. "After that, we ruled out all of the East Coast," Jackie says, "because it was too expensive. Besides, we didn't want cold weather. We wanted warm." The next step in their search was sending for information on retirement opportunities in Florida, Georgia, Louisiana, Mississippi, and Alabama. Alabama, which has a program that actively recruits retirees to live there, was the only state that sent them information about what it would actually cost to retire there. "The others just sent us tourism information," Jackie recalls. "So we wrote to three different areas of the state, visited them, and then chose one."

The choice was based on affordability as well as on amenities. The first cost they looked at was taxes, Gary says, "because that's a very fixed expense." In their last home in Ohio, Gary and Jackie paid about $1,200 a year in property taxes. Before that, in New Jersey, their property tax bill was $3,600. Now they pay $225 a year for a three-bedroom, three-bath house, with seven and a half acres and four hundred feet of lake waterfront. They bought their house—now it's worth about $300,000—when it was a one-room fishing cabin, and added on to it. But Jackie, a real estate agent, says that in the surrounding county, comfortable homes are available for about $54,000 and up.

Utilities for their all-electric Alabama home come to about $13 per month for water and $70 for electricity, including heat. In Ohio they were paying about $400 a month for electricity. And—except for groceries, which cost about the same—Jackie says expenses such as dining out are also much less than up north.

Gary and Jackie could not be happier with their choice. "Alabama sent us one brochure that talked about 'a beautiful remote community on a seventy-five-acre lake with one hundred people,'" Jackie recalls, "and Gary said, 'That is where we are going to live.'"

That's where they do live now, and Gary and Jackie are so happy there that they've become professional boosters: She is a real estate agent and he works as a volunteer, ushering around visitors who come to the area looking for a beautiful and economical place to retire.

#45

For Your Retirement Home, Choose a State with Low Property and Income Taxes.

While we're working, we may grouse about paying taxes but not put too much effort into reducing them. But when the time comes to retire, and income tends to flatten out, taxes become a much bigger factor in your budget. The couple in this story did not focus on choosing a low-tax state when they first decided to retire. But their story is an object lesson for people who are trying now to catch up on saving for a future retirement: You may not need to play as much catch-up with your savings as you thought, if you're willing to move to a state where you can reduce your annual tax bills by several thousand dollars.

Norma and Brent, now sixty-seven and seventy, respectively, made a snap decision to retire to a town in North Carolina in 1985. His work with a U.S. government agency had taken them to live in various countries in Asia and Africa. They had vacationed on the coast and in the mountains of North Carolina and they found the state beautiful. "So when we found a house we liked, we bought it and moved there," Norma recalls. "But it was a mistake. We hadn't done any research and we sort of blindly bought a house and settled in."

Soon the negative aspects of their choice began to surface. About seventeen miles from a major town, "the little area where we lived was hardly even a village. Every time we wanted to go shopping or any time we wanted to go to see the symphony, it entailed driving. And as we got older, we realized we were driving thirty-four miles to see a movie." Along with transportation, other daily costs of living mounted as more retirees moved to the area.

And so did the taxes. "Property taxes became a big factor. We got very little relief from the state government. And then county taxes started going up as well. We were living on a fixed income. As all these taxes increased, it meant that we could afford to do less and less," Norma explains. They started to search in other southern states for another retirement location—an area with a full-service golf club, which was important to Brent, as well as one with lower taxes.

After visiting venues in the Texas Hill Country and some areas of Arkansas, Georgia, and Florida, one day they noticed an item in *Money* magazine about the benefits the state of Mississippi offers to retirees. Norma and Brent admit that they were skeptical at first: Their image of the state did simply not comport with their vision of comfortable retirement living. But they responded to the advertising blurb and received both written information and a series of phone calls from volunteers who participate in "Hometown Mississippi," the program designed to attract residents. "We had a lot of questions about the medical services, the cost of living, the traffic situation, and of course the taxes," says Norma. One particularly attractive feature was that Mississippi exempts retiree income—including Social Security, private and government pensions, and annuities—from state income tax.

Their interest piqued, Norma and Brent traveled to Mississippi and decided to settle in a college town that shows its respect for the older newcomers—among other things—by offering a program of short-term, low-cost courses on topics such as computer skills and the Civil War, to retirees. The sale of their four-bedroom house in North Carolina produced enough proceeds to buy another four-bedroom home in Mississippi for the same price. But the new home is "much nicer, with a better location, and the yard is better landscaped," Norma says. In addition to gaining a better house, they've cut utility bills by about a thousand dollars a year.

What really makes a difference in their retirement budget, however, is Mississippi's low taxes. Brent estimates that now they are saving $2,000 a year in state income tax, and about $1,000 a year on property taxes (they pay about $825, compared to $1,850 in North Carolina). Added to lower utility costs and a generally lower cost of living, the tax breaks have been a major factor in reducing financial pressure on this retired couple. And besides, now they have to drive only four miles to go to the movies.

#46

Trade the Higher Cost of City Living for a More Economical Life in the Country or in a Small Town.

If you've lived most of your adult life in the city or in a suburb, it may be difficult to imagine living in a town without a Starbucks, a subway system, or a symphony orchestra; or hunkered down in a cabin in the woods where a woodstove plays an important role in winter heating. Yet many retirees who strike out and try this lifestyle end up loving it and surviving on a lower retirement income than they thought was possible.

For many years George worked for a member of Congress on Capitol Hill. He lived in a comfortable two-bedroom condominium apartment in downtown Washington, D.C., where "the general lifestyle of the city I was accustomed to was expensive." That lifestyle included buying a lot of books and eating many meals in restaurants instead of preparing them at home.

Before going to Capitol Hill, he held a series of jobs in the arts field, but "I paid no attention to retirement. I only put away money for retirement when I was required to" by his employer. "I apparently thought I was just going to go on forever without saving," he says.

Finally, around 1985, he was forced by the rules of his employment to contribute either to Social Security or to a government pension plan. For that, George is grateful. After all, despite his inattention to retirement, he has achieved a goal many of us can only envy: He took early retirement at age fifty-two. "For retiring early, I took a 6 percent annual cut in my pension. But I didn't really think of my new life as retirement, though. I thought of the pension as a guaranteed income that would keep a roof over my head—a way that I could go off and get paid for doing things I really wanted to do, to be my own boss."

George was forced by his job to catch up on saving for retirement. But equally important in making his retirement affordable was realizing that he could fashion a congenial lifestyle in the country and live on a lot less income than in the city. This change of perspective occurred when a friend of George's built a home in a small town about an hour and a half outside Washington, in West Virginia. After visiting his friend, George was intrigued enough to rent a house for a summer, and then for a year. After many enjoyable weekend getaways, "I was pretty well sold on country life. I realized it was affordable, and that even if I couldn't get some consulting or other work, I could still keep a roof over my head."

A big factor in the affordability of his new venue was lower taxes. As soon as he decided to move, George transferred his official residence from Washington, D.C., to West Virginia, saving about $300 per month in withholding from his last few months of salary. He also sold the condo and bought a house on two acres two miles outside of the town he'd chosen. As a result of the move, George's property taxes declined from about $900 per year in the city to $350. And as a recipient of a federal pension, George benefits from an extra $2,000 deduction on his state income taxes.

The income tax deduction is especially useful, since George has continued to work part-time as a self-employed consultant and part-time executive director of a nonprofit organization. He made major improvements to his house with the profit from selling his city condo, but the work income has enabled him to afford additional improvements to the house, as well as treat himself to splurges such as an occasional meal in a top restaurant and even a trip to Tibet. "People who are retiring should consider not taking a part-time job, but doing something—such as consulting—that gives you a beneficial tax status," he advises. "I was able to reduce my taxable income significantly with deductions for a home office, transportation and other work expenses."

When he retired, George rolled some money he'd saved in his Capitol Hill retirement plan into IRAs. He still hasn't used the money, because withdrawing it before age fifty-nine and a half will incur a 10 percent penalty. But in the last year or two, George has taken a breather—he has not decided if it's permanent or not—from even his part-time work. So when he turns fifty-nine and a half in a few months, he plans to start using income from those savings to help pay his regular expenses.

This is one retiree who seems to have done everything right: He loves his new home and community, he lives on a much smaller income than when he was working, and he does not feel deprived in any way. "I surprise myself on a daily, weekly, and monthly basis," George marvels, "when I think about how your life can work out when you do what you want to do and the pieces come together."

47

Look for a Location Where You Can Build on Your Interests and Skills to Create a Simpler, Less Expensive, but Satisfying Way of Life.

Retirement may be the time when you want to indulge in a pent-up desire to travel on luxurious cruise ships, eat at fine restaurants, or tee off on world-famous golf courses. Or it may be a time when what you really desire is to simplify your life, to shed financial responsibilities for others without feeling guilty, and to find pleasure in activities such as gardening. Moving out of the city to a location where you can have a large garden can reduce many living expenses as well as nourish you with healthy, home-grown food at a bargain price.

Marian, fifty-seven, has a background in academia and works now as a self-employed textbook writer. She's lived and worked in Taiwan and in Oman, one of the United Arab Emirates, and she has a teenage son. For many years she struggled to pay the bills and was unable to pay for health insurance, let alone save money for retirement.

Just about three years ago, Marian started earning $60,000 a year in royalties from the sale of her textbooks. This enabled her to start catching up on her saving for retirement. The additional income has also spurred her to research incorporating her business, which she believes will increase her tax savings—for example, allowing her to deduct all of her medical expenses—and to contribute as much as $30,000 per year in a retirement plan for herself.

About three years ago, Marian's new financial success also prompted her to start thinking seriously about the financial aspects of creating her ideal retirement lifestyle. She hasn't filled in all the details yet, but—because there is no guarantee that the royalties will continue to flow at the current level—over the years she's been embellishing her vision of how she might live comfortably on limited financial assets. Total retirement, which she defines as termination of paying work, is not on the agenda, "until I'm forced into it by illness or decrepitude." But once her sixteen-year-old son has finished college, Marian plans to launch a new lifestyle for herself—one that's based on living in a rural setting and taking advantage of its natural assets. She will start by selling her present home in Virginia and moving "to very cheap housing—maybe even a mobile home (but not in a park!) a little farther south, say, South Carolina—to save on heating." To cut down on the future costs of her food, she explains, "I have started to garden extensively, and I'm wondering how much of my own food I could raise." As a prelude to "returning to vegetarianism and freezing a lot of garden produce," she's enhanced her skills by taking courses in horticulture, master gardening, and "edible landscaping." The idea behind edible landscaping, she explains, is instead of planting ornamental trees, cultivating fruit trees; or instead of choosing ornamental bushes, planting blueberry or cranberry bushes, all of which can help reduce her food budget.

"Please understand that I don't see these plans as deprivation in any way. I would much prefer to live frugally," Marian explains, "and trade the money for time. . . . As long as I have my garden, my pets, and a beautiful natural environment I feel rich."

#48

Consider Living in Another Country.

How strong is your sense of adventure? If saving enough to retire comfortably in your current location seems impossible, moving to another country with a lower cost of living could be both exciting and economical.

Victor, age sixty, holds joint citizenship from Canada and Australia. This is a man who took the plunge to live overseas about thirty years ago. Now he's considering doing it again: returning to North America from halfway across the world—but this time to live in Mexico, not in Canada.

Victor has family who live in California and he'd like to be closer to them. But living in Mexico will be much less expensive than living in California. This self-employed psychologist has enjoyed the years he spent living in the tropics and in one of the major cities Down Under. But two years before he is eligible to start receiving a pension from the government, he acknowledges, "I live pretty well and so haven't saved much. Besides," he adds, "I have lost money on various silly real estate and stock market ventures over the years."

Victor's pension is so low that he might not even bother to collect it. How can that be? The Australian government provides the pension "to all oldies if they are eligible," he explains. But the amount you receive is docked if either your assets (including your home) or your income exceeds certain limits. "The only way to get around this," Victor says, "is to invest in pension annuities [not counted by the government as income]," which don't have a high yield.

Currently Victor is saving several thousand dollars a year with the goal of increasing his assets to about $200,000 U.S. But if he meets his goal, he estimates, the total income he could receive from the government pension would be about $250 to $300 per week "if I'm lucky."

That's where the Mexico vision comes in. Victor has enjoyed traveling in Mexico. He also thinks that by locating in an area with a lot of other "gringos," he could generate income by continuing to practice part-time as a psychologist. Here's how this scenario would work financially: Victor would give up his Australian pension and instead keep the $200,000. He would spend some of the money, perhaps $50,000, on a small apartment, and invest the remainder in "higher-yielding equity funds" to produce a stream of income. With about $300 per week from his practice and $250 per week in investment income, he figures that life in Mexico could be very pleasant. After all, Victor says, he's been reading about the low cost of retirement in Mexico on various websites and has already corresponded with "retired folk" in Ensenada, the town he's considering—and has even heard of "one couple who are living in Puerto Vallarta on around $600 per month."

TIPS

☑ **If you're considering moving to a less expensive town, region, or state, contact the governmental authorities for information on the costs and benefits of retiring there.** If you don't know where else to begin, write to the office of the governor and ask to be referred to the appropriate agency. Internet surfers can usually locate some relevant information by searching under the name of the state. Here are the contact points for Alabama's and Mississippi's retiree attraction programs, which are referred to in the examples above:

- Alabama Retiree Attraction Program: 800-235-4757

- Hometown Mississippi: 601-359-3607

☑ **Before choosing a new location for retirement, compile a list of the characteristics you are looking for, and also determine the limits of your budget.** Then see how the locations you are considering measure up to your criteria.

☑ **To avoid costly mistakes, don't move to a retirement location without first visiting and, ideally, spending enough time there to get a feeling for the lifestyle, as well as the cost of living.**

☑ **Know the ramifications of your tax situation if you plan to move.** To get an overall picture of tax treatment of retirees by various states in the U.S., check out:

- The National Association of Retired Federal Employees at www.narfe.org. Click on "Legislation Directory" to see "State Tax Treatment of Federal Annuities." This section lists state sales and income tax policies as well as treatment of retirement income. To make sure you have current information about taxes, contact the state or county to which you are considering moving.

If you retire outside the United States, your tax obligations to the federal government and to the country where you are living will be determined by international tax treaties. For information on rules that affect retirees living in a particular country:

- IRS Publication 901, "U.S. Tax Treaties." To order, call the agency at 800-829-3676, or look it up on the Internet at www.irs.ustreas.gov.

☑ **Consider becoming a snowbird.** To get advice on how to be a snowbird, you can find numerous websites by simply searching "snowbird" on the Internet. In addition:

- *The Canadian Snowbird Guide,* a book by Douglas Gray

- http://www.snowbirdguide.com, which offers extensive tips aimed at New Yorkers who spend the winter in Florida (such as how to avoid double taxation), but will give you an idea of issues to consider for snowbirding anywhere in the U.S.

CHAPTER NINE

MONITOR YOUR RETIREMENT RESOURCES

Surprises: That's a theme that surfaces over and over as people talk about catching up on retirement savings. Most of the surprises people relate are negative ones, but there are also some positive stories.

The negative surprises are the wake-up calls: the realization that if you don't take conscious steps to catch up soon, either you'll have to work to pay your bills for the rest of your life, or you won't be able to live in the retirement style to which you want to be accustomed.

When they occur, the positive surprises are truly wonderful. These surprises usually materialize when people finally start paying attention to their financial situation and realize that their assets are larger or more flexible than they thought, or that their retirement goals really are attainable now, or at least soon. The story of Jenny in Chapter 3 illustrates this phenomenon. This realization may come as a surprise because of lack of knowledge about retirement planning, saving, or investing. Or it may occur—as it did in Jenny's case—because you've simply been living day to day and not paying attention to your finances.

By definition, positive surprises are good and negative ones are not.

But when it comes to retirement saving and planning, even a positive surprise can have a bad side: By not focusing on your retirement, you may have already lost time and opportunities to change your lifestyle or pursue personal goals that you've been putting off.

This book started by recommending an initial assessment of all the resources that potentially could help support you in retirement. The first chapter suggested where and how you could look for those resources to make sure that none would be overlooked. Subsequent chapters described some of the many strategies employed by Americans from a wide spectrum of work and family experiences to take control of their retirement finances. These included making a plan for saving and spending, as well as building on existing assets by accelerating savings and reorganizing or investing them.

This section of *The Retirement Catch-Up Guide* focuses on how you can implement the final step: monitoring your retirement finances—and progress on your plan—to make sure that you really are catching up, rather than just treading water.

There's no single ideal way to do this monitoring. What's important is to create a system that works for you. However, there are certain basic elements you should include in your monitoring to give you an accurate picture of your progress:

- Your salary or other earnings. If you change jobs, or if your self-employment or small business has a very good year or a very bad one, you may need to adjust your plan and assumptions.

- Your savings rate. Are you actually sticking to your plan to put a certain percentage of your income, or a flat amount, into retirement accounts? If not, why not? If you're actually saving more, how does that affect your future estimates?

- Your investment earnings. Are your retirement, savings, or other brokerage accounts generating the income you have been counting on? If not, perhaps it's time to reorganize your portfolio—or to take some money out of bank accounts and invest it in mutual funds with a greater return.

- Other assets. These include your home, perhaps a piece of investment or vacation property or a share in a business. Are they increasing or decreasing in value? Do the changes in value suggest new strategies for maximizing your retirement resources?

To monitor these key financial factors, you can create your own system or find one in a money management book or by searching the Internet, or by consulting a financial planner. You might use the Internet to keep track of your investments, but also create a notebook or filing system that will allow easy reference to key documents—such as bank statements, reports on your 401(k), or your Social Security Statement—that arrive in hard copy.

Whatever the system, it should be simple and straightforward enough that you will take the time to maintain it and to use it to make midcourse corrections.

#49

Keep Your Mind on Retirement Financing, Even When You Have Little or No Money to Devote to It.

Most or all of the jobs you have will ultimately contribute to your retirement income, whether through Social Security, a pension, or personal savings. So you should always be as aware of what's happening to your retirement resources as you are of the bills you have to pay next week. The more conscious you are of shifts in your financial situation, the better prepared you will be to adjust and maximize whatever resources are available to you.

Abby and Dick, both in their mid-seventies, have led one of the most unpredictable lifestyles imaginable: For decades they've been in politics, uncertain from one term to the next where they might be living and how much income they would have, let alone how much money they'd have for retirement.

He served in elected positions on the state and national level. Although she never ran for election, in addition to raising six children, she was always active in local politics and in his campaigns and she also worked as a public official and an advocate on a variety of political issues.

Although Dick was a member of Congress at the time, when Abby was almost fifty years old, they realized that they would not be able to pay for college expenses as well as retirement unless she shifted from unpaid to paid employment. When Abby applied subsequently for jobs in the government and in academia, she asked for a salary commensurate with what she would have received if she'd been properly paid for her work in the political arena, and succeeded in getting the amount she requested.

If you'd asked Abby twenty years ago exactly how much money she and Dick would need for retirement, she could not have given you a dollar figure. Over the years, she says, "I made no specific calculations about planning for retirement, only general ones." On the other hand, retirement was always on her list of financial concerns. In the 1960s she took a class in money and investments at the YWCA, and learned about mutual funds before she even had the money to invest in them. Years ago Abby set up a family budgeting system with subaccounts in the bank, so that she could predict and manage expenses such as income taxes, investments and charitable contributions. With retirement in mind, periodically she requested and received a copy of both her and her husband's Social Security accounts, estimating the potential size of their benefits. She and Dick started IRAs as soon as they were created, and continued to contribute to them throughout their careers. "I feel I invested too conservatively," Abby says, looking back, "but who knows? The stock market could have plummeted." Although a congressional pension was optional when her husband was in public office, he signed up for it, and she made sure that she would be eligible for survivor benefits from the pension.

Dick began to collect his congressional pension when he was sixty, but with a history of longevity in both of their families, they decided to continue working and to delay taking their Social Security benefits until they were seventy. Even now, they fill their time with speaking engagements and teaching and writing activities that also help pay their living expenses and for such necessary treats as visiting grandchildren and even lending money to their children to do things such as buy houses and start businesses.

Abby and Dick were not always sure that they would have enough resources for a comfortable retirement. With a large family and careers that were hard to predict, they can attribute their financially successful retirement to two key factors: Abby's re-entering the full-time paid workforce at age fifty; and throughout most of their lives, constant vigilance over all of their financial matters.

"In many ways I think of the early part of our retirement like my days as a mother—I needed to generate some income and keep watching our finances and prepare for the long life ahead of us." When Abby says "the early part of our retirement," she means now. Abby's mother is ninety-five, and Dick's father lived into his nineties. She figures that they have another couple of decades of retirement ahead of them, so she is not about to abandon her vigilance of their finances any time soon.

#50

Monitor Your
Investments on the Internet.

The Internet has put both planning and managing
retirement finances within the grasp of anyone who
can learn to hunt and peck on a keyboard. Even if
you are leery of buying or selling stocks, bonds, or
mutual funds on the Internet, you can keep track of
how your investments are doing, up to the minute, if
you are willing to pay a relatively small fee to subscribe to certain brokerage services.

"I watch the stock market on the Internet every day," says
Roberta. "But that doesn't mean I do anything" every day, she
explains. "I am not a panic person."

Roberta's sixty-three and she has postponed starting on
Social Security until age sixty-five so that she will receive a
larger benefit. For twenty-five years she and her husband Sam
operated a small wholesale business, selling items for hobbyists
and teaching people how to use the materials and tools. They
always tried to put money into Simplified Employee Pension
plans (a tax-deferred retirement savings account) for themselves and their employees. "But there were good years and
bad years, and it wasn't possible for us to contribute in the
later years" that they operated the business, Roberta explains.

For several years, Sam was ill and unable to participate
fully in the business. So about five years ago they started

thinking about retirement. When they examined their small portfolio, they realized that some stocks they had bought twenty years before simply were not worth holding any longer. They started to reorganize their portfolio to increase the earnings, but when Sam died three years ago, Roberta did not have a specific retirement plan. So she was responsive when a buyer appeared and offered her a decent price for the property where the business was located. Her goal was to invest the proceeds of the property sale successfully enough to support her until she's sixty-five and starts taking Social Security.

With the help of her son, who works in an Internet field, Roberta decided to take advantage of the new technology, which also allows her to save on brokerage commissions. To track her investment progress, Roberta has set up her portfolio on the Internet and created spreadsheets that help her figure out if her own holdings are performing as well as she needs them to. Not one to act on impulse, she carefully studies the market, taking advantage of the availability of "competent information almost without cost" that she can read on the Internet.

Roberta gets her information from Internet sources including free e-mail services such as Standard & Poor's and www.infobeat.com, financial news and management sites such as www.zacks.com, and the websites of the mutual funds she owns.

Sometimes her research and her monitoring system prompt her to buy or sell an investment. "For example, sometimes I have a mutual fund that is stagnating. I had one a year ago that was well rated. But other equity funds like it were going up and this one was not moving," so she sold it and bought a fund that was performing better. Using Internet spreadsheets and calculators, "I keep percentages and calculations on my holdings. If something that is comparable has gone up 12 percent and mine has only gone up 6 percent, I turn it around and put the money into a different fund."

With no job and no Social Security, Roberta says, "I am more or less dependent on my investments. My goal is basically to retain the capital and get some income out of it." Although she checks her portfolio every day, Roberta says that about once a month she takes a more detailed look to make sure "that my principal is working in some small way." She actually trades only every couple of months. So far the Internet strategy is working for her. "If I invested a lot of money in help [from a broker], that would be money that's gone down the drain. If people are willing to take the time and effort on their own, it's not difficult."

In a way, it may be too easy. Although this is not a problem for her, Roberta cautions that "it takes a lot of discipline to stick to your original ideas and not get carried away with the ease of trading and the munificence of free advice to change the way you invest." Her advice to potential Internet investors: "Remember that only you are responsible for your investments. . . . Think before you click."

#51

Read All the Statements You Receive from Your Pension Fund, 401(k), or IRA to Catch Mistakes Before It's Too Late.

Do you really know exactly what's happening with your retirement savings and investments? It's tempting to ignore the fine print, to say nothing of all those numbers, on monthly or annual account statements. But both human beings and computers can make mistakes. A serious mistake, or one that is compounded over time, can cost your retirement funds a lot of money if you don't catch it.

Like many American families, Grace and her husband Alan did their best to contribute to IRAs at the same time they were raising a family and even paying for the children's high school and college educations. But when Alan died two years ago at age sixty-eight, Grace, who was then fifty-six, suddenly had to focus on her retirement finances in a much more concentrated way than ever before.

Grace and Alan had married when she was twenty-eight and he was forty. She'd worked for a few years as a research scientist, and he had been a government clerk before opening a neighborhood bookstore in Baltimore. The bookstore provided the family's basic support, but as their four children grew older, Grace took a course in interior design and began to work part-time to help pay some of the children's private school tuition. They started putting money into IRAs when a regular customer of Alan's who was a broker came into the shop one day and suggested that they take advantage of this new form of tax-deferred retirement savings.

For many years the broker managed the IRAs for Grace and Alan, who did not pay much attention to the investments. When the broker retired, they had accumulated about $120,000 in the IRAs and $70,000 in utility stocks. On the advice of friends, they shifted these assets to another brokerage we'll call Acme Investments.

In the meantime, Alan's health had been declining severely. For many years he was depressed, and eventually he was diagnosed with a degenerative chronic disease. With the decline in his health came a decline in his bookstore business. "I knew that we had to get out of the business, and also move out of our high-rent district in the city," Grace recalls. After more than two years of searching for a rural location that would be near both mountains and water, in 1996 they settled a few miles outside a small college town in Virginia. They used the proceeds from their home in the city to buy a house and ten acres of farm property.

By this time Alan was receiving Social Security retirement benefits and also making withdrawals from his IRA, which they were using for daily expenses. Every month Grace was receiving "massive computer printouts—worse than a telephone bill" about their accounts with Acme Investments, but she really did not know how to decipher them. "I grew up in the home of a southern gentleman who believed that women should not concern themselves about money," she explains. "If I ever asked a question about money, he would say, 'Don't worry your pretty little head about it.'" The new broker did not seem motivated to help educate her either. "He answered my questions if I asked, but he did not offer any advice or assistance," Grace says.

Then, in 1998, Alan passed away. "The IRA withdrawals and the Social Security stopped abruptly," says Grace, but that was only the beginning of her financial challenges. She had been devoting a lot of her time to caring for Alan, and was earning only a tiny income from her occasional interior design work. With the $60,000 life insurance payment Grace received, she kept $30,000 for the year's living expenses and, on the advice of the Acme broker, invested the rest in an annuity.

After Alan's death, for no apparent reason, the utility stock dividends "I had been receiving like clockwork for twenty years stopped coming. Then when I got the tax records, they showed a huge disbursement to me—$200,000—on which I was going to have to pay income tax of about 30 percent." The $200,000 represented the approximate total of funds in both her and her husband's IRAs. When she inquired about the utility stock dividends, she learned that "some message in some computer" had started depositing them in a separate account instead of sending them to her every month. No one at Acme could explain how this happened. When she started thinking about the huge tax bill she would face for the IRA funds, Grace concluded that the government "would not do that" to a widow, and started questioning Acme Investments about their paperwork. The Acme broker was slow to respond, coming up with a series of excuses for why he could not explain what had happened to her account. After several months of frustration and delays, Acme finally acknowledged that instead of crediting the IRA funds to Grace's account and recording the $200,000 as a disbursement, they should simply have rolled over her husband's IRA so she would not have to pay taxes on it.

After this experience with Acme, Grace was determined to start learning more about managing her own retirement resources and to find a more trustworthy adviser. She attended free seminars on issues such as estate planning and "investments for the mature investor," offered by various financial services companies, and also met with several prospective advisers. She finally chose an independent local self-employed financial planner who inspired her confidence by taking the time to help her better understand her financial situation. One of the things he pointed out was that the annuity purchase was a bad financial decision because it would not even begin to pay off for at least eight years, and carried a severe financial penalty for pulling out of it. Grace liquidated the annuity, paying a $2,000 penalty to do so. "I took a bath on that," says Grace, "but he convinced me that getting rid of it was the right thing to do." The new broker has also earned her trust by suggesting that the stodgy investments in the IRA portfolios be replaced with a diverse group of somewhat more aggressive funds—all of them no-load, so she will save money on commissions.

For the adviser's services, she pays an annual fee of 1 percent of the value of her portfolio. The fees that Acme charged her, she says, "I honestly have never been able to figure out," despite repeatedly asking for explanations. What she does know is that Acme charged 1 percent of the value of the IRAs, 2 percent of the value of taxable investments in their accounts, and "additional fees for other specific circumstances that were never made clear to me."

Grace is fortunate that she and Alan were able to save as much as they did in IRAs. But she also realizes that, although she grows a lot of her own food and lives frugally, she's likely to need additional resources to ensure her security for many years to come. For Grace, then, catching up on retirement savings starting at age fifty-eight really encompasses three strategies: building up her business to increase income, "husbanding my resources" by keeping her living expenses down, and managing her investments to build them up as much as possible before she starts withdrawing money for her retirement.

And, not to be forgotten, for Grace, catching up also means taking more responsibility for her own financial future.

#52

Compile a Quarterly Report on Your Retirement Savings.

Most businesses compile quarterly reports on their financial status, so why shouldn't families or individuals do the same thing? Whether you use some type of financial software or your own makeshift format, this can be an effective way to keep from straying from your retirement path.

Maggie started to compile a quarterly report summarizing the family's finances about a decade ago when she had to apply for a loan for her small business. The bank required her to prepare a statement of assets and liabilities. "Once you start," she says, "it's just a wonderful way" to stay on top of your cash flow, your savings and your assets.

Another prime motive for doing the quarterly reports was to make sure that she and her husband Buck would save enough money for their two children's college expenses. When she started keeping records, Maggie set up a report form in Word computer software. She created sections to keep track of the college fund, the value of their home, their investments, their debts. In 1994 she added a "retirement summary" where she kept track of their retirement savings and other relevant information such as the benefit estimates they received from the Social Security Administration.

Now, at the respective ages of fifty-two and fifty-five, Maggie and Buck plan to work another decade until they retire. Her field is social work, and his is education. Thanks at least in part to her reporting system, they have succeeded in saving $100,000 to pay their two children's college expenses. Maggie never doubted that they would succeed. "I didn't have the panic attack about college expenses that my husband did. I could see from the quarterly reports that we were on track."

Now that Maggie and Buck have met the college funding goal, they are focusing on catching up on retirement savings. Over the years they have accumulated about $285,000— partly in IRAs and partly in other brokerage accounts—that they plan to use for retirement. After years of passive investing, "we have decided to be much more active in this phase, to loosen up and go for investments that will produce a better yield. My husband has the portfolio on his computers at work and home," and he communicates regularly with his broker about investment decisions. They have already benefited considerably from the bull market. In 1999, she says, the value of each of her own four IRA funds increased between 40 and 98 percent. Having recently sold a business that was not doing well financially, Maggie has taken a new job. Now she puts 12 percent of her salary into the 403(b) plan [similar to a 401(k), for employees of nonprofit organizations]; her husband has recently doubled his contribution to his own 403(b) to 14 percent of his salary.

Even as they have accelerated their savings, Maggie says her husband Buck is worried that they will not catch up to meet their retirement goal—to generate 80 percent of the approximately $150,000 annual income they are earning now. With a conservative assumption of growth in their current retirement savings, Maggie estimates, they are already at the 60 percent mark, which would provide them with $1,900 per month less than their goal. She knows that they could probably live on a lower income, but "although we don't live lavishly, we like to travel," she says; and they might also want to maintain two residences—one in a northern climate and one in a warm climate.

Because Maggie pays such close attention to the numbers, she is confident that even if their gains in the stock market slow down, they will have enough to live on when they retire. That's because her retirement account records already show the following good news: that when her husband is sixty-six, they will be eligible for at least $5,200 and possibly $5,800 per month from his pension and their Social Security. And most heartening of all: These are figures that—if they change on the quarterly reports—will always go up, never go down.

#53

Check In with Your Financial Adviser Once a Month.

Busy people who cannot or do not want to put a microscope to their retirement finances every day may legitimately depend on a financial adviser to do that for them. But your money is still your responsibility. One way to minimize your anxiety—especially if you are depending heavily on investments for retirement—is to make a point of getting a monthly update.

Carl, who is sixty-four now, worked hard for many years to build his small international trade business. By age fifty-two he'd put about $200,000 into a retirement plan. When the company's profits began to increase significantly, he went to a Dan, a financial adviser, for help in planning his future. Over a few years, they worked together to establish the value of the business and, ultimately, to sell it. When he sold the business, Carl became a consultant and continued to earn a good income, both from his new work and from receiving payment for his company over a period of time, rather than all at once.

Before seeking professional advice, two factors were slowing down his retirement savings: spending on luxuries, especially vacation trips to places such as Europe and various ski resorts; and a weakness for "hot" investment deals that did not always work out well.

Dan helped Carl set up a plan that allowed him to put away more than $100,000 per year in pensions and other retirement savings. But Dan also told him that to achieve his goal of accumulating $1.8 million for retirement, Carl would also have to rein in his impulse spending and investing and live on a budget. "We made an agreement that he would not spend any more money than was in the budget. We set a road map for his savings."

Carl's trying hard to stick to the road map, and he's succeeding. He and his wife have decided that will limit their monthly spending to $9,000 per month. She keeps the family accounts, using financial management software on her computer. They have vowed not to make purchases without consulting with each other, and they have improved their financial situation by cutting back on expenses such as renting a boat slip for a boat they were not using and selling property that was generating a tax bill.

And, perhaps most important of all, Carl takes an active interest in monitoring the investments that constitute their retirement savings. Often he calls Dan to see how he's doing. But he also has requested a monthly summary statement of all of his investment accounts, showing their combined rate of return, comparing it to the performance of other market indicators, and illustrating where the account stand in relationship to the goal of saving $1.8 million.

Carl is not sure exactly when he wants to retire, where he wants to live, and whether to continue working as a part-time consultant. His uncertainty, however, is to be envied. That's because there is also certainty—the knowledge that he will be able to choose almost any lifestyle he wants. Carl knows this because the reports he's receiving on his investments show that when he turns sixty-five a year from now, all of those options will be open to him, because he has almost met his goal of having $1.8 million to support him and his family.

#54

Make a Comprehensive Pre-retirement Checkup of All Your Resources.

In our complex financial world, it is easier than you might imagine to lose track of money. So even if you think you know where all of your savings and assets are, it could be worth the trouble to do a thorough inventory again as you are on the verge of retirement.

Meredith is seventy-three and her husband, Vince, is seventy-four. They've been retired for about a decade, and most of that time they've been trying to figure out how to live comfortably on a limited income.

Meredith was a music teacher and Vince is a pharmacist who enrolled in a seminary, intending to become a minister. When a hospital in India heard about him, they convinced the couple that Vince could make a greater humanitarian contribution helping them set up a pharmacy than he could as a preacher, so they moved to India with their three children. As missionaries, they earned small pensions from the church. But for twenty years after their India experience, Meredith and Vince changed jobs and moved several times and did not accrue any retirement benefits.

As retirement age approached, they sold their house in Florida and bought a thirty-five-foot trawler. For about two years they lived in the boat, teaching themselves how to use it. Then for four years, they plied the waters of the Caribbean. Afterward Meredith and Vince planned to "buy a houseboat and tie it up in a marina near Fort Myers, Florida," she says. But the fees to rent a boat slip, plus other living expenses, were more than they could afford on their limited retirement income of about $1,500 a month from Social Security and a few hundred dollars more from pensions and a few investments. While trying to identify an alternative place to live comfortably on their income, they visited a daughter who lives in the Washington, D.C., area and researched the cost of living in the nearby eastern panhandle of West Virginia. "West Virginia's a beautiful state, the cost of living is reasonable, and it's within two hours of Washington, D.C.," Meredith explains.

So instead of living in a dreamboat in Florida, they moved to a cabin in the woods, about a mile and a half from the road and three hundred yards from their closest neighbor. In recent years they've made ends meet by continuing to work—Vince as a part-time pharmacist and Meredith by playing the organ at local churches.

Then one day Meredith received a letter from a long-time acquaintance of her family, saying that Meredith's name had appeared on a list published in the newspaper of "lost" people who had accounts with the State of Wisconsin. She called the toll-free phone number in the ad and was informed that they were holding a pension for her that dated back to her tenure as a music teacher in a rural school district about forty years before. She recalled that the school system's contribution to the account had been around $600. "They asked me how I would like to receive the money—in a lump sum or whatever," she recalls, "and I asked them how much money we were talking about. They told me that it was $22,000. I was amazed." Meredith and Vince gave $1,000 to each of their grandchildren and have invested the rest to help pay their own expenses.

The windfall could be an important boost for them at a time when Vince is having serious health problems and they are considering moving again—this time to Florida, to live in a mobile home park.

What they really don't want to think too much about is how much more that pension might have been worth—and how the value might have kept up with inflation—if they'd collected the money and invested it sooner.

TIPS

☑️ **Make a commitment to read all of the financial statements you receive every month.** These should include statements from your bank, credit cards, investment accounts, and reports on retirement accounts such as your 401(k). If there is something you don't understand, question it and insist on a prompt answer or a correction, if appropriate.

☑️ **If you don't do it already, consider monitoring your investment portfolio on the Internet.** There are dozens of options for doing this free, without even opening a brokerage account or using the Internet to trade. They include Microsoft Excite, American Online, Yahoo!Finance. Along with stocks you already own, you can watch stocks you might want to buy in the future.

☑️ **Private sector employees who have a pension, including defined contribution plans such as a 401(k), are entitled to receive an individual benefit statement that describes your accrued and vested benefits every twelve months.** If you do not receive a statement automatically, request it from your employer or plan manager in writing.

☑️ **Get all your unclaimed money.** To search for a pension you may have earned from the public sector, or a bank account or other financial resources you may have forgotten about, contact the agency for "unclaimed property" in your state capital or look on the website of the National Association of Unclaimed Property Administrators (www.naupa.org).

☑ **Take a snapshot of your retirement savings status.**

- Use the Profit Sharing Council of America's "Annual Retirement Checkup" form, available on the Internet at http://www.psca.org, or by calling the organization at 312-441-8550.

☑ **Keep abreast of the market value of your home.**

- Check with local real estate companies, read the real estate ads for comparisons, or look at http://www.HomeGain.com for lists of recent sales of comparable homes in your neighborhood.

ACKNOWLEDGMENTS

The people I most want to thank and acknowledge for their help are those who told me their stories on the condition that their real names would not be used in this book.

But a number of other experts and colleagues have also been especially helpful in compiling both the data and the personal stories in *The Retirement Catch-Up Guide.*

Several of these are public affairs officers whose quick and complete responses to my many queries are especially appreciated. They include: Carolyn Cheezum and John Trollinger, Social Security Administration; Chuck Mondin, United Seniors Health Cooperative; Danny Devine, the Employee Benefit Research Institute; Sharon Morrissey of the Pension and Welfare Benefits Administration, U.S. Department of Labor; and Tom Otwell, AARP.

Other experts and colleagues who have also been generous with their help and encouragement include:

Arvonne Fraser, a writer, speaker, and women's rights advocate in Minneapolis, Minnesota; Douglas Gray, author of *The Canadian Snowbird Guide;* Duke Grkovic, a financial adviser who is based in Richmond, Virginia; Judi Campbell of Women in Technology in the Washington, D.C., area; Lois Finkelstein, a lawyer in Bethesda, Maryland; Maryellen Gor, a professional trainer and consultant in Frederick, Maryland; Martha Priddy Patterson of Deloitte & Touche in Washington, D.C.; Paula Monroe, a tax preparer and investment adviser in Park City, Utah; and Tom Corliss, a California real estate agent who founded the Senior Advantage Real Estate Council.

For their editorial and general professional support in making this book a reality, I thank my agent, Noah Lukeman;

editors John Jusino and Grace Farrell; and Newmarket Press president, Esther Margolis.

Last but not least, I want to thank the two main men in my life for helping me keep my work on target: my retired father, Milt Hoffman, who continually urges me on to the next project by asking me "What are you working on now?" and Riccardo Accurso, who never lets me forget about the importance of our own retirement planning for very long.

INDEX

Personal Finance/Retirement Books From Newmarket Press

ELLEN HOFFMAN

The Retirement Catch-Up Guide
54 Real-Life Lessons to Boost Your Future Resources Now!

Real stories. Real people. Real strategies. Here's how these late starters made up for lost time and how you too can catch up on your financial planning for retirement.

"A jam-packed guide filled with commonsense advice, countless resources, and personal anecdotes."—Don Blandin, President, American Savings Education Council

Bankroll Your Future Retirement With Help from Uncle Sam—2nd Edition
How Government Perks and Policies Can Affect Your Income, Your Healthcare, Your Home, and Your Assets

"An invaluable resource for every American planning for a secure retirement."
—William V. Roth, Jr., Former Chairman, Senate Finance Committee

SUZE ORMAN

You've Earned It, Don't Lose It ®
Mistakes You Can't Afford to Make When You Retire

Over 500,000 copies sold! Orman's only book specifically on retirement, this covers investment advice, trusts vs. wills, joint tenancy and gifting, power of attorney, long-term-care insurance, early retirement, and more. From the author of the #1 *New York Times* bestsellers *The Courage to Be Rich* and *The 9 Steps to Financial Freedom*.

Books are available from your local bookstore, or use this coupon. Enclose a check or money order payable to **Newmarket Press** and send to: Newmarket Press, 18 E. 48th St., New York, NY 10017. Credit card orders: **1-800-669-3903** or **1-800-233-4830**

I enclose a check or money order payable to Newmarket Press in the amount of _____

Name _____

_____

Address _____

_____

_____

City/State/Zip_____

E-mail_____

quantity	title	amount
	Bankroll Your Future Retirement, 2nd Ed.	
_____	$16.95 pb (1-55704-462-7) . . . .$	_____
	The Retirement Catch-Up Guide	
_____	$14.95 pb (1-55704-518-6) . . . .$	_____
	You've Earned It, Don't Lose It	
_____	$15.00 pb (1-55704-316-7) . . . .$	_____
_____	$24.00 hc (1-55704-322-1) . . . .$	_____
_____	$19.95 audio book (1-55704-285-3) .$	_____
	*Plus shipping and handling .$	_____
	NYS Residents add 8.25% Sales Tax .$	_____
	TOTAL AMOUNT ENCLOSED .$	_____

*Shipping & Handling. Add $3.50 for the first item, and $1.00 for each additional item. Allow 4-6 weeks for delivery. Prices and availability are subject to change without notice.

For discounts on orders of five or more copies or to get a catalog, contact Newmarket Press, Special Sales Department, 18 East 48th Street, New York, NY 10017; phone 212-832-3575 or 1-800-669-3903; fax 212-832-3629; or e-mail sales@newmarketpress.com

BOB.RCUG.0402